The Anti-Depressant Book

Praise for The Anti-Depressant Book

"Dr. Jacob Towery has been a great friend and colleague of mine for many years. In this, his first book, he offers a radically new perspective on the treatment of depression in teens and young adults. Whereas many 'self-help' books focus exclusively on one or a few approaches to recovery, Dr. Towery recognizes that individuals are unique and there's no such thing as a 'magic bullet' or panacea that works for every person. Mood is influenced by many independent factors, and this book offers insights into finding the right combination of approaches to achieve sustained recovery from depression. These approaches include cognitive, motivational, interpersonal, behavioral, spiritual, and meditative practices, along with healthy exercise habits. I wish more child therapists and psychiatrists followed this approach to treating their patients with depression!"
—Matthew May, MD
Adjunct Clinical Faculty, Stanford Department of Psychiatry

"In this book, Dr. Towery combines his unparalleled experience with treating adolescents using the most cutting-edge psychological treatments for depression together with a direct, no-nonsense yet compassionate style of teaching and writing. His respectful, practical, and goal-oriented guidance in this book makes depressed teens accountable for the work needed to overcome depression. His treatment approach is systematic, clear, and wise, making this book easy to follow and extremely useful. I would want my teen struggling with depression to read this book."
—Maor Katz, MD
Director of the Feeling Good Institute

"Jacob Towery is my favorite adolescent psychiatrist. He is a seasoned clinician with a knack for simplifying the complex. In this book, he has created an owner's manual for the teenage brain, as well as a troubleshooting guide for those suffering with mood and anxiety difficulties. I am grateful that he has taken the time to disseminate his most effective strategies in a compilation of self-help techniques."

—Kim Bullock, MD
Clinical Associate Professor, Director of Stanford Neurobehavioral Clinic

"Dr. Towery has an approachable, honest, and witty style that allows readers to connect to the life-changing messages in this book. He consistently addresses the lack of motivation experienced by many youth with depression and supports them in making changes. Dr. Towery compassionately pushes readers toward turning their lives around."

—Angela Krumm, Ph.D.
Adjunct Clinical Faculty, Stanford Department of Psychiatry

"The Anti-Depressant Book is a great book (and workbook) for teens suffering from depression. It is also an excellent guide for their parents who just want to help and wonder, 'What can I do?' The book makes working with cognitive behavioral therapy easy and approachable. It really focuses on ways to help people feel better in real time. It is a wonderful addition to my library and a great resource for my patients and their families."

—Alexander Strauss, MD, DFAACAP, FAPA
Clinical Assistant Professor, Department of Psychiatry at Robert Wood Johnson Medical School

"The Anti-Depressant Book is a fantastic resource for teens struggling with depression and the parents who support them. Dr. Towery highlights the active ingredients that will help your teen fully recover from depression, including: increasing sleep and exercise, mindfulness, cognitive therapy techniques, and gratitude exercises. Dr. Towery balances the need for self-compassion with careful accountability in this must-read, practical self-help book for teens with depression. If your son or daughter is struggling with depression, I highly recommend that you hurry up and get this book for them—it just might save their life!"

—Jill Levitt, Ph.D.

Adjunct Clinical Faculty, Stanford Department of Psychiatry

The Anti-Depressant Book

A Practical Guide for Teens and Young Adults to Overcome Depression

and Stay Healthy

By Jacob Towery, MD

Jacob Towery, MD, is an adolescent psychiatrist in private practice in Palo Alto, California. He attended Duke University for his undergraduate studies, University of Virginia for medical school, and Stanford for his residency in adult psychiatry and fellowship in adolescent psychiatry. He currently serves on the Adjunct Faculty at Stanford University School of Medicine. He enjoys snowboarding, scuba diving, traveling, reading, and spending time with the people in his life.

Table of Contents

Acknowledgments

So, this section could easily be about 47 pages long. While that would satisfy my desire for thoroughness and indulging in gratitude, it might be quite boring to you, the reader. So, I'll attempt to make this a bit more concise, but no promises. How to even start? Chronologically?

First off, mom and dad. Thank you for conceiving me, not abusing or neglecting me, and giving me lots of love. Mom, even though you push my buttons more than any other human, I appreciate your love, support, and generosity. Dad, you are one of my most significant role models in life. Although I encourage you to cut back on your work, I admire your work ethic, your intellect, and your integrity.

Thank you to Alex, my brother, for helping steer me indirectly into psychiatry and for modeling discernment and stability. I am proud of you!

Thank you to my numerous teachers growing up who inspired me to learn, think hard, and spend decades in school. A few who come to mind are Stan Heard, Mr. Hunter, Sandy Stark, and Michael Montague-Smith.

Thank you to my friends from high school through now who

taught me that the people and relationships in life are more important than the objects: Vishal Sahni, Garrett Griffin, Stephen Pfleiderer, Yaron Oren, Jim Poulos, Eli Reiman, Alex Strauss, Matt May, Maor Katz, Zach Huselid, Ryan Brown and Ryan Zaklin, Shannyn DeBlaauw, and James Starke. More recent friends, supervisors, and colleagues who I care about and inspire me to do therapy within a community of wonderful people include Edna Esnil, Jill Levitt, Helen Yeni-Komshian, Ali Darcy, Carlos Greaves, Kara Fitzpatrick, and Linda Lotspeich.

Special thanks to David Burns, my main mentor at Stanford, who taught me how to be awesome at TEAM therapy and inspired me to teach a lot, be generous, and explore all the amazing things that the world has to offer.

For this book in particular, I'd like to thank my amazing research assistant, Marcelle Friedman. She found everything remotely related to statistics and research and saved me all that work and did so on a tight deadline. Thank you, Marcelle! My editor, Becky Hall, has been outstanding. I have never actually met Becky in real life, and it is a testament to her professionalism, work ethic, and easygoing nature that I hired her without an in-person meeting. So far, I have been thrilled with this choice! Anna Hirsch, my friend and cover art creator, is stupendous. Thank you, Anna, for putting up with my changing ideas for the art, coming up with really cool ideas yourself, and making it happen! Shout out also to John Brearton, my friend from "Honesty Salons" who came up with the awesome title of the book that far surpassed my title ideas. Thank you to Angela Krumm for reading the book in advance and giving me many wonderful suggestions for how to improve it. Thank you to Kim Bullock, Matt May, Alex Strauss, Maor Katz, and Jill Levitt for reading the book, offering thoughts, and writing a blurb. This book was truly a team effort!

Thank you to Alexandra Havrylyshyn for giving me the book *The Clockwork Muse*, which inspired me to write the whole book in 20 two-hour sessions over six months and for generally being supportive and wonderful.

He won't be able to read this right now, but thank you to my son, Bryce, for putting up with the many afternoons I picked him up later than he wished so I could write and edit this book. Bryce, I will try to do a better job of picking you up earlier now, and I love having you as my son! I couldn't be a luckier father.

Finally, thank you to my past and future patients. You have shared with me the most intimate details of your lives, trusted me to steer you in positive directions, worked your butts off to make changes, and allowed me a tremendous sense of satisfaction, joy, and connection. I truly can't think of a career I would rather have and feel incredibly fortunate to get paid to do something I love. Thank you!

Introduction

This book was almost never written. I don't consider myself an impressive writer, nor do I particularly love writing. After I first decided to write this book, I was excited about the project for approximately one week, then did absolutely nothing with it for about six months and essentially gave up on it. I'm thrilled that I ever actually started the book, let alone finished it.

The main reason that I ultimately decided to write this book is that there was an epidemic of suicides in my hometown of Palo Alto. Five teenagers killed themselves on the train tracks in the first five months of 2015. And this wasn't the first suicide epidemic here. Five teenagers from Gunn High School died by suicide between May 2009 and January 2010 while I was doing my pediatric psychiatry fellowship at Stanford (Green, 2015). I was called in as one of the consultants to Gunn following those suicides, and everyone was panicked. Shockingly, these deaths comprise just a small proportion of recent suicides in the area: between 2009 and 2011, 26 teenagers in Santa Clara County took their lives, in addition to 35 young adults between the ages of 20 and 24 (Ojakian & Mukherjee, 2012).

1

As an adolescent psychiatrist, I felt somewhat helpless hearing about one suicide after another among teenagers in my city. I enjoy seeing teenagers and young adults, and it is very satisfying helping those who are depressed get better. But in traditional one-on-one therapy, there are only so many people I can see at a time. It has been horrible getting calls from desperate parents wanting treatment for their children, not having time to see more patients, and knowing that most of the other high quality therapists around here are also full.

Many of the best depression self-help books out there are written for adults. Other self-help manuals are wonderful for small children. But I wanted a book written specifically for teenagers and young adults with depression that I could refer these families to and prescribe as part of my treatment. When I looked around, I came up short.

So, I decided to write this book. I wanted it to be practical, easy to read, and not too long (this one was a big struggle, given my natural wordiness). I wanted it to be low on theory and high on concrete tips, so you could get results within several weeks. I wanted a book that was specific enough that you could do exactly what it suggested and not be overwhelmed. I wanted a book that was interactive; helpful for those

2

who are mildly, moderately, or severely depressed; and in an ideal world, even fun. And I wanted it targeted specifically for teens and young adults still living at home so that it was relevant and useful.

I am grateful to my many teen and young adult patients who allowed me to write about their lives. I have changed identifying information for anonymity, including names, genders, hobbies, ethnicities, and other details.

If you have had times when you've struggled with depression, you have probably had moments when you felt hopeless and like nothing would make any difference. I feel quite hopeful that if you read this book cover to cover and follow what it says, your depression will go away and likely never return. I know this might sound corny, but if even one young person reads this book and gets rid of their depression or doesn't commit suicide as a result, this book will have been incredibly worth it to me. Thank you for giving it a chance.

Jacob Towery, MD
Adjunct Clinical Faculty, Stanford University School of Medicine
& Department of Psychiatry

How to Use This Book Effectively

This book is not like other books you've read. Although it might be enjoyable to read at times, it is not designed for pleasure reading. This is not a novel best read by the pool in one afternoon, nor would I recommend consuming a few pages as you drift off to sleep, only to be forgotten by the next day.

This book is meant to change your life. And I want you to take it seriously. If you only intend to skim the book, or read the chapters that suit you, or read it passively, you might as well throw it in the garbage right now. Reading it any of those ways will waste your time, and you will get nothing out of reading it. I'm serious. I don't want to waste your time.

My hope is that if you are reading this, you are a teenager (or their parent) who has suffered from some form of depression and really wants help. I wrote this book for you. But you will only get anything out of this book if you use it properly. If you race through the book, ignore what it says, and change nothing in your life, by the time you finish you will be just as unhappy as you are now. Nothing will change, and you will say that this book sucks. I don't recommend that option. Instead, I recommend that as you go through this book, you keep in mind three principles that will allow you to get a lot out of this book and make it worth your time and energy. Sound reasonable? If you don't want to follow all of these principles, I genuinely suggest stopping the book now and finding another option, because this book will only help you if you use it effectively.

Principle #1: Interact with the book.

This will not come naturally to some of you. You may have grown up hearing that books are to be treated very carefully, never dog-eared, underlined, or written in. If you are reading this on an electronic device, there may be technical limitations to doing anything other than reading the words. Or, more commonly, you may find it taxing to write in a book and may resent being asked to put this much effort into a book, particularly when your energy is already low. Any of these sound familiar?

Well, I've got good news and bad news for you. The good news is that I can't make you do anything you don't want to do. So, if you decide not to interact with the book, I can't stop you. The bad news is that if you are stubborn on this point and don't do the written exercises, you won't get much out of the book. You probably won't change any of your behaviors, and you won't feel any better. I could be wrong, and you can test this out by going through the book and avoiding the written exercises, but you will likely be wasting your time. Also, since I am strongly recommending you do ALL of the written exercises, if you don't do them, and then you feel crappy, please don't say that the book "didn't work." OK? My hope is that if you do the written exercises (and follow the next two principles), you will start to feel significantly better within the next few weeks. Only then will we be able to accurately say whether or not the book "worked" for you. Fair?

If you are reading a paperback or hardcover, by far the easiest approach is to just write directly in the book itself. Feel free to underline parts that resonate with you, write in the margins, highlight; do whatever allows you to engage with the material and retain it better. This will save you needing to carry around a separate notebook that you might lose or forget to bring to a therapy session. It will be easy to find your answers, and all you'll need is a pen or pencil.

The more challenging situation is if you are reading this on a

Kindle, iPad, or other electronic device. Depending on how much the device allows you to "write" in it, you might choose to write the answers in the text. If this is fairly user-friendly, I say go for this option. However, at least in 2015, there is no easy way to do this, so I recommend that if you are reading this on an electronic device, buy a small notebook with a pen attached that you keep in your pocket/purse/bag at all times, and put all your answers in the notebook. I recommend that this notebook be somewhere between 3 to 8 inches across and 4 to 11 inches long. I found one on Amazon that looked pretty good, so you are welcome to just purchase this one if you like:

http://smile.amazon.com/Wellspring-Flip-Antique-Honeycomb-FlipNote-AntiqueHoneycomb/dp/B00QVWCXQA/ref=cm_wl_huc_item

Note: I do not have any financial ties to either Amazon or Wellspring, I don't know if this link will continue to function in the future, and if you are reading this far beyond 2016, you may not even recognize this "Amazon" thing that I allude to.

I have had clients that used dozens of loose pieces of paper and tried to stuff them in their backpack, which made finding those answers challenging and added a lot of clutter. If you don't own a small notebook that has lots of empty pages, now would be a great time to set down this book and either go to a drugstore and buy one or order one online with two-day shipping or less. Then, after you have done that, feel free to come back to this book.

When in doubt, try to be actively engaged with the reading, including doing all of the written exercises. You will get much more out of the book.

Principle #2: Read this book daily when you are somewhat alert.

For many books, it doesn't matter how much you read at a time or how often you pick them up. There are certainly upsides to reading this book over only a few days or on a long plane flight. What are those upsides? Go ahead and list some of the advantages of reading this book all at once or over a few days. Don't turn to the next page until you've listed at least two advantages.

1. _Retain information better (maybe)_

_____

2. _More likely to follow principles / stay motivated_

3. ___can use/apply skills faster___

4. ___will help reduce anxiety/depression___

5. ___will help relieve symptoms___

6. Able to see results faster/understand yourself better

7. Would be a good kickstart/beginning to seeking resources for mental health

Hi. Did you list at least two advantages on the previous page? If so, well done! You're interacting with the book. Excellent. If you did not list at least two advantages of reading the book all at once, please stop and go back and do this. Really. Then we'll continue.

Have you now listed at least two advantages? If not, you may want to pay careful attention to the chapter coming up on "Good Reasons to Hold On to Depression." I won't get into it too much here, but if you're already trying to cut corners, this doesn't bode well for success. There's still hope, though. Just go back to the last page right now and list two advantages, and then we can start fresh for the rest of the book.

OK, by this point I'll assume you listed at least two advantages. Well done. What did you come up with? I can think of a few advantages to reading this all at once or over only a few days:

1. It's faster.

2. You won't have to deal with reading it later.

3. You can start putting the ideas into motion right away.

4. You have the free time now and might not have it later.

5. You haven't read for a little while and you're seeing your therapist tomorrow, so if you read 100 pages today, you'll be

"caught up" and won't have to explain why you're behind.

Any of these sound familiar? You may have also come up with some advantages I didn't think of. That's great.

On the other hand, there are also some advantages to reading this book every day at a slower pace, perhaps ten pages per day. More like the tortoise than the hare. What are some advantages to reading and interacting with this book in more regular chunks? Please don't turn the page until you've listed at least two advantages.

1. _Process ideas slowly / at your own pace_

2. _Adapt to schedule better_

3. _Don't feel rushed_

4. _Reading fast could lead to missing out important details_

11

5. stay on habits/coping mechanisms longer

Hello. Did you come up with at least two advantages on the last page? If not, please go back and do that. I won't get into the same long-winded rigmarole as two pages ago, but it's the same principle. You won't get much out of this book if you just try to "do it in your head" or read it passively. Trust me. I've had clients do this, and they are the ones that don't get better. Don't let that be you. Go back and write down two advantages.

Welcome back. Thanks for writing down at least two items. What did you think of? Here are the advantages of reading the book daily that I came up with:

1. You will retain the material better. [Tangent: I love explaining the concept of "chunking" to my clients. It usually takes a couple of minutes, but in essence the idea is that the brain remembers chunks of material (like "650-415-2222") better than a long string of individual numbers. Also, the brain tends to remember the first part of what you learned in a book or lecture ("primacy effect") as well as the last thing you see/hear/read in a movie/paragraph/chapter ("recency effect"). This means that the more "chunks" you have when you're learning something, the more beginnings and endings you have, and the better you

retain the material in the long run.]

2. In some ways it's easier than reading it all at once.

3. The book might help make you feel hopeful that things can change, and you can experience that daily rather than once or a few times.

4. You might feel accomplished each day that you did something to improve your situation.

5. Many of the behaviors and skills I'm going to suggest you change and learn will work best if you do them over several weeks, rather than over one or a few days.

In my opinion, this last point is the most important reason to read the book slowly. For example, it's quite challenging to change sleep and exercise habits all at the same time and immediately, particularly if you are also learning new cognitive strategies. Instead, you are more likely to be successful if you focus just on sleep for a little while, and then focus just on exercise changes. In fact, in a perfect world, if you were not pressed for time and your mood was wonderful, I would have you ONLY focus on changing your sleep for an entire month until your new sleep habits became routine. And then, once those changes were ingrained in your schedule, you would focus exclusively on regular exercise for a month, then exclusively on meditation for a month. The advantage of this strategy is that your new habits would be more likely to stay ingrained and less likely to get dropped. In fact, if your depression is on the mild side and you're not in as much of a hurry to change things, you could consider (ideally talking with your therapist or counselor about this idea, if you have one) pacing your reading schedule such that you give each of these three above-mentioned chapters their own month and work really hard on making each of those behavioral changes individually.

For other readers, my fear is that waiting several months to get into any of the cognitive strategies might be too long and lead to unnecessary suffering. Furthermore, I'm nervous that your momentum is high right now, and if we space this book out over six months or so, the momentum might go down, particularly if you're not seeing a lot of progress. So, for many readers who read several pages of the book per day, there will be some overlap between behavioral changes while they are still becoming a habit, and I apologize for this. For future editions of this book (and I love suggestions, feel free to contact me if you have ideas), I will try to think of a way that allows for daily reading of the book and still gives a month per behavioral change. Still working on it for now. But, in essence, reading the book over a few weeks at least allows you some time to change multiple behaviors (and not all at once) and increases the odds of you retaining the material. So, please consider sticking to the recommended ten pages per day rather than taking the all-at-once route.

Principle #3: Do what the book recommends.

I know this is a big request. You've probably never met me. We don't have any relationship other than what you think of me from reading this book so far. You might be wondering if I'm worthy of your trust or if I'm a snake oil salesman promoting some sham. I can sympathize with your skepticism. There are a lot of frauds out there and a lot of people with ulterior motives trying to get you to give them money or do things that are in their interest rather than yours.

I'll try to be upfront here. I do want to be worthy of your trust, and I don't want to come across as defensive. The fact that I'm charging more than zero dollars for this book shows that there is a financial aspect. I am hoping that some people will buy this book, and I might even make a profit from it. But, if you have already paid for this book, then I'm not going to make any "extra" money from it whether you do what I recommend or not. My main goal here is that I want you to actually get some relief from your suffering. I spent many years at Duke, University of Virginia Medical School, and Stanford learning about depression in teenagers and how to treat it effectively. I have seen hundreds of young adults with depression, including dozens who were suicidal. I have seen them get better with these methods and often recover completely within weeks. I want to help you feel better quickly, potentially without even needing to see a therapist.

But there is nothing I can do to help you if you ignore what I recommend. It would be like going to a personal trainer to lose weight, listening to them talk about changing your diet and exercise, learning how to do the exercises, but then never exercising or changing what you eat. That's an ineffective way to lose weight.

Same thing here. You can read about sleep and exercise and meditation and cognitive strategies, but if you don't implement the changes effectively, nothing will actually change in your life. You won't feel better.

On the other hand, if you do what I recommend in these

17

chapters, I genuinely believe you will feel significantly better. Even if you

feel hopeless. Even if you are miserable and thinking about killing

yourself. If you read these chapters and do what I recommend, you will

start to feel better and get results quickly. I've seen it work for people

who were probably even more ill than you. But, you actually have to DO

what's in the pages—not just read about depression. Make sense? Are

you in? OK, let's begin.

Depression

Depression affects millions of teenagers and young adults around the world every year. To give a sense of just how many suffer from depression in the United States, about 20% of adolescents will have a depressive episode by the age of 18 (Lewinsohn et al., 1993). Depression makes people hopeless, causes misery, and worst of all, it causes thousands of people to kill themselves every year. In fact, depression is the most common psychiatric disorder among people who die by suicide (Harwood et al., 2001). According to a study in Finland, as many as 59% of those who die by suicide have depression (Henriksson et al., 1993).

In addition to the personal suffering it causes, the economic costs of depression are also high. Depressed individuals miss more work than non-depressed workers (Kessler et al., 1999), and they are less productive at work. In fact, depression impairs performance and focus even more than chronic physical conditions do, like back pain, headaches, and arthritis (Wang et al., 2014). In total, the 2010 economic burden of adults with depression in the U.S. was estimated to be $210.5

billion (Greenberg et al., 2015). Billion with a "b." That's a lot!! Although there is not nearly as much research on teenagers with depression as adults, my person experience suggests that depressed teens experience a lot more academic trouble than their non-depressed peers. They tend to miss more school days while depressed, get lower GPAs, and have a harder time getting into college. Those same teenagers are often bright and do much better when their minds are clearer.

The personal and economic tolls of depression are clearly enormous. To make matters worse, many teens with depression never seek help for this illness. For those that do look for professional help, there is often a shortage of qualified therapists and adolescent psychiatrists.

Let's start with defining "depression." According to the DSM 5, (for better or worse, this is the book in psychiatry and psychology that defines what every mental illness "is"), someone has "Major Depressive Disorder" if they have had at least one "Major Depressive Episode" lasting at least two weeks (for those under 18, the duration only needs to be one week). Symptoms of depression include feeling sad, loss of interest in daily activities, sleeping more or less than usual, feeling guilty or worthless, low energy, trouble concentrating, increase or decrease in appetite, moving slower than usual, and thoughts of suicide. To meet criteria for a Major Depressive Episode, you must have had at least five of these symptoms, with one or two of those symptoms being a sad mood and/or loss of interest in daily activities.

Part of what makes diagnosing depression challenging is that it can look very different from one person to the next. Sometimes it's easy to diagnose. For example, Beth, a 16-year-old girl, was referred to me by her therapist because her mood was still low after several months of treatment. Beth was very likeable. She dressed differently than other girls her age, she gave up a spot in the popular crowd when she realized they were more superficial than she anticipated, she was a musician, and she was an idealist. But, over the past few months she had stopped enjoying hanging out with her friends and playing guitar, she was sleeping poorly, she'd gained some weight, her energy was down, her parents sometimes found her crying in her room, and she was fighting frequently with her boyfriend. Things had gotten so bad that she had thoughts of killing herself.

Beth was clearly depressed. Thankfully, she was diagnosed quickly, and within a few weeks of us working together, her mood improved dramatically. She stopped needing therapy with me after about 12 weeks, and she's now significantly happier, playing guitar again, and has found a new group of friends that she feels closer to. She just informed me last week that she got straight A's last semester and is enjoying life a lot more now.

Other cases can be harder to diagnose. Sometimes people can look depressed, when the primary culprit is really anxiety. Once the anxiety is treated, their mood lifts, and no further treatment is needed.

In other cases, people can look perfectly happy and still be profoundly depressed. For example, I recently started seeing a 17-year-old young man named Matt. He had been depressed for three years almost continually, but because he had such a convincing smile and knew how to say the things people wanted to hear, he flew under everyone's radar. His pediatrician was shocked when he found out how down Matt really was and sent him to me for diagnosis and treatment. What was interesting, from my perspective, was that Matt never cried, he still had friends, still played basketball, but internally he was miserable and had been forcing himself to "go through the motions" for the last several years without really enjoying anything.

Fortunately, Matt was very motivated to get out of this dark place, and we did several two-hour sessions every week for about four weeks. He started sleeping more, meditating regularly, and learned how to change his thoughts. Slowly his mood scores began to consistently improve. We probably still have one or two more sessions to go and then Matt will be on his way, but his smile is now starting to match his internal state. The treatment remains the same regardless of how the depression presents, but the challenge here was that Matt looked happy to those around him and went undiagnosed for a long time.

Another challenge with depression is that sometimes it can be over-diagnosed. Some parents and counselors, in a good-hearted effort to be vigilant and not miss signs of an important illness, can assume teens or young adults are "depressed" when they are experiencing normal bouts of sadness.

One of my favorite clients was Sarah, a 13-year-old girl whose parents brought her in for treatment of "depression." Sarah's grandfather was from Dubai and built a very successful oil business, her parents owned a private jet, and their family took frequent vacations to Maui and Switzerland. Sarah had a flair for the dramatic and had an intricate social life. When one of her friends announced that she was terminating their friendship, Sarah told another friend, Jackie, that she was going to kill herself. Jackie was understandably worried and told several other friends, some of which told their parents, who called Sarah's parents. Pretty soon many people were scared and worried about Sarah.

I only met with Sarah three times. On the first two visits, I was struck by how charming and vivacious she was. Sarah was a remarkable storyteller. She was excited about her upcoming summer in Dubai, nervous about a boy she liked but curious to see if it would go anywhere, and she lacked any of the common symptoms of depression, such as changes in appetite, sleep, energy, concentration, etc.

Now, Sarah certainly had times when she felt sad for hours at a time, and she would sometimes cry during these episodes and look for comfort. Minutes later, she might be laughing or talking excitedly about something at school. Her parents were understandably worried about these "mood changes," particularly in combination with the threat to kill herself.

However, when I asked Sarah about her desire to end her life, she was quite frank that she did want to live but she was very upset about losing a friend and was mad at that girl. She knew that threatening suicide would be upsetting and hoped the friend would feel sorry for her and resume the friendship.

24

The good news here was that Sarah did not suffer from clinical depression. She had changes in her mood that could last several hours, but this is normal for most teenagers (if not everyone) and by itself does not mean much. I educated her parents about what signs to look for should she develop depression. In our third and last session, I also talked with Sarah about pros and cons of "threatening suicide." She said that she liked talking to me, but she had a lot going on in her life so it made more sense to find other, more skillful ways of repairing friendships, and she agreed not to use this threat in the future. Her parents emailed me a few months later to say she was doing much better and there had been no further threats.

At this point you might be wondering whether or not you are depressed. Or, if you are clearly depressed, how severe is it? You can find out right now by taking a three-minute self-assessment called the Patient Health Questionnaire (PHQ-9; Spitzer et al., 2015). Once you start incorporating some of the tips in this book, you can also use the PHQ-9 to track which symptoms are improving and which may be slower to change (Löwe et al., 2004). For each question, you will give yourself a score of 0-3, which reflects how frequently you have struggled with a given symptom in the past two weeks (0=not at all,

1=several days, 2=more than half the days, 3=nearly every day). Then you will check off the appropriate box for question 10, which reflects how severely your symptoms have impaired your ability to function socially, academically, and personally.

Feel free to take the PHQ-9 test below to see where you are right now. In case you want to take the test once a week to assess your progress, I've included a blank version of the PHQ-9 at the back of the book (in the Appendix) so you can photocopy that one. The questionnaire is also readily available online (www.phqscreeners.com).

PATIENT HEALTH QUESTIONNAIRE-9
(PHQ-9)

Over the <u>last 2 weeks</u>, how often have you been bothered by any of the following problems?
(Use "✔" to indicate your answer)

	Not at all	Several days	More than half the days	Nearly every day
1. Little interest or pleasure in doing things	0	1	2	3
2. Feeling down, depressed, or hopeless	0	1	2	3
3. Trouble falling or staying asleep, or sleeping too much	0	1	2	3
4. Feeling tired or having little energy	0	1	2	3
5. Poor appetite or overeating	0	1	2	3
6. Feeling bad about yourself — or that you are a failure or have let yourself or your family down	0	1	2	3
7. Trouble concentrating on things, such as reading the newspaper or watching television	0	1	2	3
8. Moving or speaking so slowly that other people could have noticed? Or the opposite — being so fidgety or restless that you have been moving around a lot more than usual	0	1	2	3
9. Thoughts that you would be better off dead or of hurting yourself in some way	0	1	2	3

FOR OFFICE CODING ___0___ + _____ + _____ + _____

=Total Score: _____

If you checked off <u>any</u> problems, how <u>difficult</u> have these problems made it for you to do your work, take care of things at home, or get along with other people?

Not difficult at all	Somewhat difficult	Very difficult	Extremely difficult
☐	☐	☐	☐

Developed by Drs. Robert L. Spitzer, Janet B.W. Williams, Kurt Kroenke and colleagues, with an educational grant from Pfizer Inc. No permission required to reproduce, translate, display or distribute.

Now that you have completed the questionnaire, it's time to score yourself. If you gave yourself a "2" (more than half the days) or a "3" (nearly every day) on question 1 and/or question 2, you may be suffering from depression that needs treatment. For question 10, if you selected "Not difficult at all," then you probably don't have clinical depression. For a complete self-assessment, add up all nine scores and find the depression severity category associated with your total score:

Minimal or No Depression (1-4)

Mild Depression (5-9)

Moderate Depression (10-14)

Moderately Severe Depression (15-19)

Severe Depression (20-27)

If you came out "not depressed," congratulations! If you decide to stop reading the book at this point, I won't be offended. However, even if you don't meet the formal criteria for depression, you may be interested in having more control over your emotions, having less intense periods of sadness, or developing healthy habits that will decrease your chances of ever becoming depressed.

If you came out mildly, moderately, or severely depressed, that's OK too. This book is primarily intended for you. No matter how bad your depression is right now, there is hope that things can get better. One of the reasons I love being an adolescent psychiatrist is that I see people come in who are so miserable that they want to die, and within a few weeks of treatment, they feel happy again. I know this might sound crazy, but I see it happen over and over again.

Feel free to take that depression questionnaire each week and see if the scores change for you. Hopefully, you should start to see some improvements soon, and we can track the changes over time to see if the gains stick.

3

Good Reasons to Hold On to Depression

I debated including this chapter in the book at all. Depression generally makes people miserable and causes tremendous suffering, so it seems obvious that everyone would want to get rid of it as quickly as possible and keep depression at bay forever. To suggest anything to the contrary sounds ludicrous and kind of insulting.

But, one of the things that has surprised me as an adolescent psychiatrist is that there are often good reasons why people hold on to their depression. When I was in my second year of psychiatry residency at Stanford, I started attending a weekly two-hour therapy training group run by Dr. David Burns. I knew that Dr. Burns had written the best-selling book in the world on depression for adults, *Feeling Good: The New Mood Therapy*, and I felt incredibly fortunate to be able to study with him at Stanford. I learned far more about how to do therapy from those training groups than I did in my traditional course work. I feel quite grateful that Dr. Burns took me on as a mentee, and we eventually became friends.

Dr. Burns points out that, although it can be counterintuitive, sometimes there are forces that motivate adults to continue being depressed rather than being happy. For example, let's say an adult has been depressed for several years, applies for Disability benefits from the government, and is approved to receive $2,000 per month. Let's say this person is unemployed and will continue to receive $2,000 every month as long as they are still depressed.

What would happen to this person if their depression were cured? They would no longer receive any Disability income. That's scary. I don't think most people in this situation would consciously say to themselves, "I think I'm going to stay depressed indefinitely because the prospect of going back to work sounds daunting, and it's easier to stay on Disability, even if it means holding on to this depression." But, can you see how the situation could unconsciously make someone less motivated to aggressively seek out treatment and get rid of their depression?

When I started working with teenagers in my child and adolescent psychiatry fellowship, I didn't know if this same principle would apply. I didn't know of any teenagers or young adults that received money for being depressed, so I wasn't sure if there might still be good reasons to stay ill. Then I met Ned.

31

Ned was a 17-year-old boy finishing his junior year of high school. He used to play drums and was one of the most talented artists I've ever met. Because he had been depressed for about a year when he came to see me, he had stopped playing music and was drawing very little. He had a girlfriend, Ayla, who he cared deeply for and who was also struggling emotionally. Ned fought bitterly with his parents about many topics, including how much time he could spend with his girlfriend, doing his homework and college applications, and whether or not he could drive a 1964 convertible that his grandfather had given to the family. Ned was at an alternative school where his teachers were sympathetic about his depression, so they were very lenient about making him do anything in class. For example, in English class, instead of writing, he spent most of his time texting with Ayla.

Ned's parents were at their wits' ends. They were kind, concerned, and very worried that his depression might interfere with him going to college or—even worse—that he might follow through on this threats to kill himself. For example, when Ned would ask to stay out late with his girlfriend, if they said no, he might say, "Well, if I can't be with Ayla, then I might as well not even be around at all." His parents were scared that if they said no, it could push him over the edge, so they would then let him stay out late or skip his homework.

Can you think of any "positives" that are associated with Ned's depression? What are some things that might be encouraging Ned's depression to stay and reduce the chances of him becoming healthy? Let's write some of them down. You may be tempted to do this exercise in your head, but you'll get more out of it if you write your answers down. Don't go on to the next page until you've written down at least two answers. What are some legitimate advantages to Ned staying depressed?

1. _Parents are lenient with Ned_

2. _Ned gets to talk to his gf more_

3. _teachers have lower expectations_

4. _he can take advantage of his parents_

5. _____

6. _____

7. _____

8. _____

Did you write down at least two answers on the previous page? If not, please go back and do so. What did you come up with? There are a number of valid reasons Ned has for holding on to his depression. Here are a few that Ned and I came up with together:

1. His girlfriend experiences some pretty intense lows as well. If he were generally happy, they wouldn't have this common bond.

2. Ned likes doing his own thing and not having his parents tell him what to do. If he's depressed and points out that he might kill himself if he doesn't get what he wants, he has more freedom.

3. Right now his teachers are very lax with him. If he were healthy, they might expect more from him, and he probably wouldn't be able to spend much class time texting with Ayla.

4. He's very angry with his parents and likes yelling at them. Right now, they chalk this behavior up to moodiness as a result of his depression and don't punish him. If he were healthy and yelled at his parents, they might crack down on him more.

5. Although his parents haven't yet let him drive the 1964 convertible (there are no airbags and it has old seatbelts), he is close to persuading them that driving that car would improve

his mood. If he were healthy, they might have less incentive to let him drive the car.

6. Homework and college applications are boring and challenging. Right now, few people in his life are expecting him to do these because of the depression. If he got over it, he'd probably have to spend hours on these tasks, and he's understandably ambivalent about this.

7. Ned's best friend, Juan, is very sympathetic. When Ned calls him and says he's having a rough day, Juan drops everything and comes over or talks on the phone and says kind and reassuring things. Who knows if this would still happen if Ned were generally happy.

These were just the answers Ned and I came up with in about 20 minutes. You may have thought of other good reasons that we didn't. Now, are these reasons for Ned staying depressed real or imaginary? They're completely real. Are they legitimate? Absolutely! If I were in Ned's shoes, I would feel torn about changing my depression because there are a number of really positive things that are coming from staying depressed. This doesn't mean that Ned is "faking it" or "unmotivated." It means that Ned is a smart guy and if there are a lot of advantages to doing any behavior, in many ways it makes sense to keep doing that behavior. It's not that he is being "manipulative" or choosing to stay depressed on a conscious level. It makes more sense to think of this in terms of the fact that humans are animals, and all animals respond to consequences (note that in fancy psychology language, the definition of a "consequence" is anything that comes after a particular behavior—it doesn't matter whether that consequence is "good" or "bad"). Anytime we do a behavior, and the consequence for doing it is something we like, we are more likely to do that behavior in the future, no matter what it is. If you run hard, and your coach says, "Great job," you are more likely to run hard the next time. On the other hand, if you say that you are sick, and your parents let you stay home from school and watch TV and eat ice cream, you are more likely to say you are sick in the future. Therefore, if any positive things are happening in Ned's life as a result of being depressed, all of those things reduce his motivation for getting better because they would disappear if he got healthy.

All of the above can be conceptualized as what David Burns calls "Outcome Resistance." Outcome Resistance means that if someone could press a magic button and have something be instantly different with no effort at all (such as an end to their depression), what are all the good reasons that they would NOT press that button. In a case like Ned's, there is clearly a lot of important Outcome Resistance that could make anyone reluctant to change their mood.

In fact, at one point in our first session, I said something like, "Gee, Ned, we've come up with so many advantages to you holding on to your depression, I'm confused why you would want to work with me and get rid of this?" Ned thought about this for a while. He mentioned wanting to feel happy more often, getting back into drumming, missing art, and that the hours fighting with his parents were tiring. He was honest and said that although he had some great reasons to feel better, he was ambivalent given the reasons we'd come up with earlier to hold on to his depression.

As I do with many of my patients, we ended up doing a Cost-Benefit Analysis (CBA) to decide whether or not to work on his depression. This sounds fancy but is basically a T-chart that lists the pros and cons of a decision and weighs their value in order to decide what to do.

Here is what a blank one looks like:

Thought to hold on to or Behavior to do:

_____

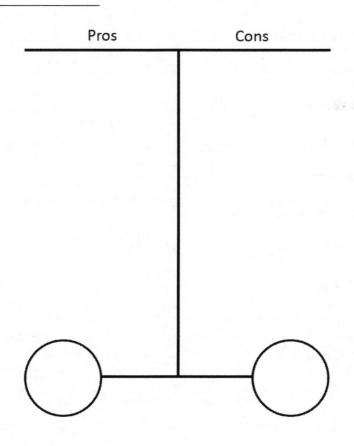

Pros   Cons

Here is what Ned's CBA looked like:

Staying depressed

Pros

1. Have more in common with Ayla
2. Parents say yes to what I want more often
3. Teachers let me do what I want
4. Parents don't punish me when I yell at them
5. More likely to get to drive convertible
6. Have a good excuse not to do homework or college apps
7. Juan gives me attention and caring

Cons

1. I feel miserable often
2. Hard to find the energy to get back into drumming
3. Not motivated to do art
4. Exhausting fighting with mom and dad all the time
5. If I don't do college apps, I won't be able to go to college after senior year
6. Counselor at school calls me in to make sure I'm OK and it's annoying
7. Grades have gone down, and if they keep going down I might not get into the schools I want
8. Feel like I'm letting my parents down

35   65

As you can see from the Cost-Benefit Analysis above, Ned had valid points in both columns. The numbers at the bottom represent how "strong" each column felt, with the two numbers adding up to 100.

When you do your own CBA, the absolute number of items in each column matters somewhat, but some items are going to be more important than others. So, it's OK if sometimes a column has less items in it but still feels stronger. Sometimes a CBA might turn out 80/20 or 55/45, but in general I recommend not choosing 50/50, as this will be less helpful in making a decision. In Ned's case, he decided that the "Pros" to staying depressed were about a 35, and the "Cons" were a 65. Since Ned's "Cons" column felt stronger than his "Pros" column, he then felt more motivated to work hard on getting over his depression.

Your situation is obviously at least somewhat different than Ned's. But the point is that if you are depressed, there are probably some very legitimate advantages to holding on to this depression that we shouldn't just ignore. In fact, one of the problems with many types of therapy is that the therapist naively assumes that the patient only has good reasons to work on getting rid of their depression and is surprised when the patient resists changing. You may have even worked with a therapist who pushed you to change and didn't honor your valid reasons for staying as you are.

Personally, as a therapist, I think it would be insulting to assume that what someone is doing or feeling is "all bad" and needs to be changed immediately. There are exceptions of course, such as if someone is actively harming themselves, but for the most part I assume people probably have good reasons to keep doing what they're doing, and it's up to each individual person to decide if they want to change in any particular way.

So, for you, I'm not going to assume that you want to change. In your situation, the advantages of staying the same might outweigh the advantages of changing. And that's OK. I'm not here to make you do anything you don't want to do, and I don't even have the power to do so. You might decide after this chapter that you would prefer to stay depressed for some very good reasons, and you're welcome to throw this book out and stay exactly as you are. In fact, I would request that you ONLY go on to the next chapter if you decide that you would be better off getting rid of your depression than holding on to it. And that's not everyone.

Let's see how this applies to you. Let's make a list of all the advantages of holding on to your depression, as well as the disadvantages. Only you can decide which column is stronger or more compelling. Your parents can't decide this for you, nor can your teachers or your friends. You get to pick whatever numbers you want

42

for each column and live with the decision.

Below is a blank Cost-Benefit Analysis. The only thing that's written on it is the decision to "Stay Depressed" or not. Please take a few minutes to write down ALL the advantages and disadvantages of holding on to your depression. This is important. Don't go on until you've done this. After you've written down all the Pros and Cons to staying depressed, read over both columns and get a sense of which side is stronger and by how much. Come up with two numbers that add up to 100 (except not 50/50) and write those numbers down under the appropriate columns.

Staying depressed

Pros | Cons

Pros

- my family is a bit easier on me?
- my friends give me extra attention
- my gf is extra nice 2 me
- teachers / ~~coaches~~ have less expectation for me
- mental illness makes me funny.
- bc of my mental illness I can help ppl more bc I relate
- familiar feeling
  - comfortable

Cons

depression is a slutbitch
- dibilitating
- its tiring having to tell ppl what's wrong all the time.
- lowers quality of my life
- can't find my actual hobbies
- can't walk my dog or be there for my dog
- makes me fill like I miss out on things/ opportunities.
- hard to maintain relationships.

(25)   (75)

__pros__

- teachers sympathize
- familiar
- less responsibility for actions w/fam
- makes me funnier
- gf gives more attention
- sisters are nicer

(30)

__cons__

- lowered motivation
- miss out on opportunities
- lowered expectations for self
- ~~not~~ self happy ~~not~~ as often
- difficult to maintain relationships

44 · sut as

(70)

How did it go? Did you come up with some arguments for both sides? Hopefully you did. Which side came out stronger? Either one is OK.

There are lots of powerful examples of Outcome Resistance that may or may not apply to you. For example, I've worked with a number of young adults who live at home and don't currently go to school or have a job. Their parents have expressed an expectation that when they are "well," they must find work and/or pay for a place to live. This can feel scary and uncomfortable to many people. In some ways, the young adult is "punished" for getting over their depression by having increased responsibility.

Another example of Outcome Resistance can be facing the possibility of someone saying, "See, it was all in your head." Some parents ask their children to "snap out of it" as if it were easy and instantaneous to get over depression. Then, if one does the hard work of getting well, it would be quite upsetting to hear someone say, "I was right. You could have just gotten over this long ago." So, an advantage of staying depressed is that you can prove the person wrong and not risk them gloating that they were right all along.

I worked with a 12-year-old girl who had seen her therapist

weekly for five years. She liked her therapist tremendously and felt a strong bond with her. She knew that when she got "well," the therapy would end. So, unconsciously, there was an incentive for her to stay ill so she could continue the relationship with her therapist.

A 23-year-old young woman that I worked with told me that she was a "mental patient" and proudly wore her armband from the psychiatric hospital she was discharged from the week before. She exclusively read books about people with mental illness and selected friends that had emotional problems. Having some kind of "mental illness" was part of her identity. She was frightened that if she got well, she would have to rethink her whole identity. We spent several sessions just talking about how scary that was and whether or not it was worth it to her to get well.

The point of all this is that Outcome Resistance for depression is real, and it's quite powerful. Once people have decided to get rid of their depression, it's often relatively straightforward and can happen quite quickly. But if we haven't fully listed and honored all the good reasons to stay depressed, then paradoxically, it's actually much harder to change.

If the Pros side was stronger for "Staying Depressed" in your

CBA, then that means that right now, you would rather stay depressed than change. That's totally fine. There is no law that says that people have to work on their depression. In fact, I've met people that have been depressed for decades. If this is where you are at right now, that's completely valid for at least two reasons. The first is that change is inevitable, and it might just be that the current events and people in your life are incentivizing you to stay depressed. This might be different in the future. You can always do this CBA again in a few days, weeks, or even months and see if the numbers stay the same or change. So, maybe another time would be better to work on your depression than right now. Secondly, even if you never decide to change your depression, you are honoring your independence and choosing how you want to be in the world, which is great.

I only have one request for you if your Pros side was stronger: I request that you own your decision. Language is important. Rather than saying things like, "I have a chemical imbalance" or "My parents are making me depressed," I request that you say something like, "Right now, given all the advantages and disadvantages, I am choosing to stay depressed." That would be more accurate. It's a different story if you read this book cover to cover, do everything it says, and are still depressed. That's different. I'm just saying that if you have already

decided that it makes more sense to stay depressed than to work on it

before you read any further in the book, own that. That doesn't mean

that this book "failed," it means that right now it's not worth it to you to

work on depression, and that's totally fine. Just own it.

On the other hand, it's possible that your CBA came out with

the Cons side stronger than 50%, and you've decided that it makes

more sense to work on getting rid of your depression. Congratulations!

It is very doable to get rid of your depression, and many people

successfully select this option. In fact, YOU are the person I wrote this

book for. My hope is that if you read this book and do everything it says,

your depression will be totally gone within several weeks. In the case

that you are motivated to work on your depression but it is so severe

that you want or need additional help beyond what is available in this

book, you may wish to see a therapist who is certified in TEAM therapy

(a results-oriented variant of Cognitive Behavioral Therapy developed

by Dr. Burns). For many of you, my intention is that this book alone will

be sufficient to dramatically improve your mood if you put in the work

and follow the instructions carefully.

But, I do have some bad news for you. There is another kind of

resistance besides Outcome Resistance, and that is Process Resistance.
Remember when I defined Outcome Resistance as the things that would
keep you from pressing a magic button that would instantaneously and
effortlessly get you what you want? Well, the bad news is that even if
you decided to go for the thing you want in spite of those reasons, I
don't actually have a magic button. There is no way to get over your
depression without putting in some serious work. If I had a magic
button, I would absolutely loan it to you. But I don't. So, even if your
Cons side was stronger and you've decided that you are willing to give
up your depression, you're going to have to work really hard for the
next several weeks to months in order to feel better. Some people don't
want to do that hard work even though they do want to get better.
That's Process Resistance.

Let me outline some of the things you would have to do in order
to get better. You would have to read this book every day, even when
you're really busy. You would have to do all the written exercises in this
book, even when you don't feel like doing them. You would have to
change your sleep habits to get eight to ten hours of quality sleep every
night. You would have to take all the electronics out of your room at
night so that you have fewer distractions while you sleep. You would

have to wake up at the same time every morning, even if you're tired.

You would have to build up an exercise regime and soon be exercising

five to six days every week. You would have to meditate every morning.

You would have to learn how to identify the thoughts that are causing

your feelings and learn a variety of strategies to change those thoughts.

In the upcoming chapters, I will walk you through all of these things and

try to help make the process easier for you, but it will still take

significant work on your part.

All of the above fall in the category of Process Resistance. The

ultimate question you have to ask yourself is, "Am I willing to do what it

takes to get better? Am I willing to put in the effort even when I don't

feel like it or don't want to?" I can't answer those questions for you.

An analogy would be if someone were overweight and decided

they wanted to lose weight and went to see a personal trainer. The

trainer might say something like, "I would be happy to show you how to

lose weight, but you are going to have to eat differently and exercise

more." You might think, "I don't want to exercise all the time or deprive

myself of foods I like. That sounds like a lot of work. But, I do want to

lose weight." Well, bad news there. If you just really WANT to lose

weight but don't make any of the lifestyle changes the trainer recommends, you probably won't succeed. But, if you DO eat healthier foods and exercise more, losing weight is actually a very likely outcome.

It's the same thing with depression. If you make the lifestyle changes that I will walk you through and learn how to change your thoughts, the studies show that you have an incredibly high chance of succeeding in feeling better. But it won't be easy. There will be many days you won't feel like waking up when your alarm clock goes off or going to school or exercising or doing your therapy homework, and yet you will have to do these things anyway in order to get better.

If you have decided that the Process Resistance is too strong and you don't want to put in the work to get better, that's OK. No one, including your parents, can "make" you decide to do the work. If you've decided that right now you would prefer to stay depressed, because of Outcome Resistance or Process Resistance or both, you're welcome to stop reading after this chapter.

Again, I have one request if you decide not to put in the necessary effort. Please choose your words carefully. Don't say, "I can't get over my depression" or "There's something wrong with my brain that's making me stay depressed." Tell people, "I have decided that I don't want to put in the work to get over my depression." That's more honest. There are fairly predictable outcomes to either decision, but I trust you to consider those and decide what you want to do.

If you have decided that you are willing to put in the work to get better in spite of the Outcome Resistance and the Process Resistance, then Congratulations! That's a big decision. I applaud you. My hope is that we can work together to get you feeling better within the next several weeks.

I don't want to sound cheesy in the next few sentences, but I've come to accept that I am kind of a cheesy person and that some of the things I say are sappy. So, here goes. I feel that I have a "calling" to help teenagers and young adults with mental health problems, including depression. I feel fortunate that I was able to train at Duke, the University of Virginia, and Stanford, and that I was able to go to school for 13 years after high school to learn these skills. I feel grateful to Dr. David Burns for teaching me incredibly powerful techniques that have allowed me to help hundreds of teenagers get better quickly. I am excited to embark on this journey with you, too. I know that sounds very cheesy, and it is, but if you read this book and end up feeling happier, more fulfilled, and living life to the fullest, that would be tremendously satisfying to me. In fact, one of my favorite things is receiving emails and cards from my former patients that have gotten

better letting me know how much they're enjoying life now. I want this

for you as well. It's totally possible. Let's get going.

Just for Parents

Note to Teenager or Young Adult: I included this chapter for your mom, dad, or caregiver in case they are interested in learning more about what you are going through and how they can help you, but if you'd rather get started learning how to feel better, feel free to skip to the next chapter.

If you are reading this, you are probably a parent or caregiver of a teenager or young adult who you suspect may be depressed. Or, they might have been already diagnosed with depression and you are looking for more help. In either case, my heart goes out to you. It can be quite painful to have a child who you know is suffering tremendously. You might be questioning your parenting skills, wondering if there was something you "should" have been doing differently. You may be feeling annoyed, or even angry with your child, as it is not uncommon for depressed people to be irritable and hard to be around. And I suspect that you may be scared—even terrified—that your child might ultimately take their own life.

This chapter was written just for you. In no way do I anticipate that one short chapter will be sufficient to adequately address all of your fears and questions. Instead, this is designed to give you a few suggestions for how to help your child and reduce any unnecessary friction between you and them.

My first recommendation may sound obvious, but I will write it anyway because it can be confusing what to do when your child is struggling, particularly if they aren't telling you much. The top priority has to be safety. If you know that your child is suicidal or actively harming themselves, you must assist them in getting professional help immediately. By that I mean a licensed mental health professional, ideally someone who has expertise and experience in treating suicidal and self-harming young people. I don't claim that this will be easy to do or inexpensive. There is a massive shortage of child psychiatrists in America (even worse in many other countries), as well as excellent adolescent psychologists compared to the demand, and you may need to call a number of people to get in with someone quickly. This is worth prioritizing. If your child is imminently suicidal, and you are not able to get in with a professional very quickly, you may want to consider taking them to the emergency room to be evaluated for safety.

You might wonder why I included "self-harming" in the last

paragraph as something to be concerned about. The reason is that individuals who deliberately self-harm (including cutting, burning, or any other method that causes tissue damage) are at a dramatically higher risk of killing themselves. In fact, a recent study published in the American Journal of Psychiatry showed that people who deliberately harmed themselves were 30 times more likely to kill themselves compared to the general population (Cooper, 2005)! This is quite worrisome. Sadly, even many licensed therapists do not know the research on self-harm behaviors and believe that this is developmentally normal, or even an appropriate response to stress. If your child is engaging in self-harm behavior and you find a therapist who is not committed to quickly eliminating this behavior, I strongly suggest you find someone else.

If you are not sure if your child is suicidal, it is quite appropriate and reasonable to ask them. There is a myth that asking people if they are suicidal "makes them" suicidal and plants an idea in their head that was not there before. This is not true. If your child seems depressed, it is better to ask them than to not ask. In fact, studies have shown that adolescents who perceive greater parental involvement and family connectedness may be less likely to make suicide attempts (Flouri &

Buchanan, 2002; Borowsky, 2001). In addition, adolescents who report feeling less able to talk to their parents about their problems are more likely to engage in health risk behaviors, including suicide attempts (Ackard et al., 2006). Although there is no guarantee that they will be honest, I have found that most teenagers have been quite forthcoming with me on this topic. Furthermore, if they tell you that they ARE suicidal, you can then take action and make sure they get appropriate help.

Other teens and young adults with mild symptoms of depression may not need or want professional help right now. That is completely fine. You may decide to simply give them their own copy of this book and see what happens. In fact, my explicit goal in writing this book is to help those depressed individuals who are not able or willing to see a therapist but really want to get better. It is also possible that your child is currently in treatment with a therapist or psychiatrist but is not as happy or as functional as they would like to be. In that case, you could also give them a copy of this book and see if they engage with it and find it helpful.

My next recommendation will probably be the hardest one to follow. Let's pretend that you have given, or will soon give, a copy of this book to your son or daughter. If you read ahead, you will probably notice that there are a lot of things the book asks of the reader, which I will henceforth refer to as "therapy homework." This includes things like going to bed at a reasonable hour, keeping electronics out of the room, exercising regularly, meditating, and learning cognitive and behavioral strategies for changing emotions. On average, the book will encourage people to spend roughly 20-30 minutes a day doing a combination of reading chapters, changing behaviors, and learning skills. My hunch is that you will have a STRONG desire to encourage your child to read the book, monitor their compliance, and nag them if they are not doing what the book says. Am I close?

Before we get to my opinion on you doing these behaviors, let's look at all the wonderful reasons for you to insist on your child reading this book and doing what it says. I would like you to write down some good reasons below. And, in the same way that I will ask your child (if they choose to read the book) to WRITE DOWN their answers, rather than do these activities in their head, it is only fair to ask the same of you. You might think that because you are an adult, you are "above" doing these written exercises. I can assure you that you will get more out of this book if you follow the instructions to the letter, including writing in it, and it will also help you have more empathy for your child when they are asked to do the same. So no cheating! Write below at least three GOOD reasons to encourage/insist/cajole/demand/nag your child to complete this book. Do not go to the next page until you have written down at least three reasons.

1. _____

_____

2. _____

_____

3. _____

_____

4. _____

_____

5. _____

_____

If you have gotten to this page and have not written down at least three reasons above, please go back and do that now! Then, return here after you have followed through. If you skip this step, you are modeling for your child taking the easy way out and cannot reasonably expect them to do anything different. So, please do the writing. Thank you!

Welcome back. There may have been a number of great reasons you came up with to make your child do the book. What were they? I will share with you a few that I thought of:

1. This is really important, perhaps even a matter of life and death. Anything that encourages them to get better is justified, and this book might really help them.

2. I have to remind them to do many things, like their homework, bringing their lunch to school, studying, going to the dentist, etc. This is just another thing they need reminding of.

3. My child used to be motivated to do things on their own, but lately their motivation has been low for everything. If I don't nag them to do their therapy homework, it won't

happen. And they need to do their therapy homework in order to get better.

4. I like telling people what to do. And I'm good at it.

5. I tried giving them this book a week ago and they have barely opened it. Maybe if I nag them to do it, they will comply and get better.

6. My child is being a jerk! They're lucky I'm just nagging them and not locking them in a dungeon.

7. I can't help myself. Nagging is just in my nature.

8. They will thank me later. I am being kind and selfless to put in the energy to make sure this happens and later they will be grateful for this.

Do any of these sound familiar? It turns out that there are many wonderful, legitimate reasons to cajole, pressure, and nag your child to read this book and do their therapy homework. In fact, I am a huge fan of you doing exactly this if it weren't for one small problem: It won't work. That's the only downside.

Getting over depression is different from learning the violin or studying for math. It has to come from an internal desire to change. If you force this process, it will probably backfire for at least three reasons. The first reason is that nagging your child to do their therapy homework will likely cause the two of you to "butt heads" and increase the tension and conflict in your relationship. Secondly, this may actually encourage your child to "rebel" by doing it in a halfhearted way, thus allowing them to defeat you and sabotaging the treatment. Finally, if you make them do this book, and they ultimately recover and feel a lot better, your involvement can undermine the sense of pride they would otherwise feel for putting in all this hard work. If they believe that it was YOU that was responsible for them getting better, they will have less of a sense of accomplishment and ownership of this transformation, and their recovery will be much more fragile.

Therefore, my formal recommendation for you at this point is to let them do this book on their own. Give them a chance. In my experience, many teens and young adults find it incredibly painful to suffer in this way, and they are often willing to put in a lot of effort if it gets them a valuable result. I have been quite impressed with how many clients I have seen recover in a short time through their hard work and willingness to take this seriously. If your child wants to feel better and is safe, give them a chance to try this on their own.

If you have already given your child a copy of this book and are wondering what to do with the energy you would have expended on nagging them, I have a few suggestions for you. The first is to check in with yourself and see how your own mental health is doing. You may need additional support beyond what you are currently getting. Many of the parents I work with have their own depression, anxiety, personality disorders, and substance problems that have not been diagnosed or treated. As you may have experienced, struggling with any of these difficulties can make it much harder to parent effectively and can put an added burden on your child. If you have any psychiatric or psychological conditions, one of the best gifts you can give to your loved ones is to get your own help. For mild conditions, this might be as simple as reading and doing a self-help book for adults, such as *Feeling Good: The New Mood Therapy* for depression or *When Panic Attacks* for anxiety. Or, it might involve something more extensive, such as getting your own professional treatment. If anything, taking your own issues seriously sends the message to your child that mental health is important and worth prioritizing.

My penultimate recommendation for you is that if your child decides to read this book and take it seriously, do what you can to make their experience more successful. For example, if they tell you they need some cash to buy "three alarm clocks," either give them the money or go buy them yourself. If your child has not been exercising adequately and they want to make this a more regular habit, support them by getting them a personal trainer for a little while if you can afford it. If a trainer for a few weeks is out of the realm of possibility, perhaps get them a gym membership or at least a comfortable pair of running shoes. If they don't have a smartphone, and you do, consider lending them your phone for 15 minutes in the morning so they can use an app to help them meditate. If you don't have a smartphone, a simple kitchen timer can be acquired for about three dollars.

Do not insist that your son or daughter tell you their innermost secrets, but do let them know that you love them and you are very available if they ever want to talk to you and get your support. Then follow through. If you are currently traveling six days a week or working until 8 PM most nights, try really hard to find a way to be home a little more so that you can have some meals together and do at least one thing every weekend together that they find enjoyable. If you have multiple children at home, your time may be spread pretty thin and you might not currently have any time built in during the week for one-on-

one time with your child. If that is the case, make it a priority to schedule at least 20 minutes a week when it is JUST you two and no one else. Do something during that time that THEY enjoy, whether it's going out for ice cream, taking a walk, or having lunch together. During that time, put your phone away. Give them your complete attention and listen to anything they want to tell you about. Do not judge, give advice, criticize, or make any recommendations. You get to practice listening non-judgmentally and empathizing with them. All of these actions show them how much you love them and pave the way for an easier recovery.

My final suggestion is one that you will hopefully never need to follow. If you have read and done all of the above recommendations, my hope is that there is a decent chance your child will decide to get help and follow through. My dream is that, particularly if they have mild or moderate depression, if they read this book and follow through completely, this will both get them out of their depression and give them the skills they need to prevent another episode. It is also possible that they will want professional help and that, with or without this book, that help will be sufficient. If in doubt, I recommend making an appointment with someone with a very high level of certification in TEAM therapy who has experience with clients your child's age. If you do not live near one of these therapists, many of the best clinicians offer "Intensives" in which you can come in for a week or two and get many hours of therapy in a short time. These can be incredibly effective in much the same way that immersing yourself in a foreign country for a few weeks can advance your language skills as much or more than months of a weekly language course.

The area that is by far the most challenging for parents is what to do if your child is very depressed, functioning poorly, but not wanting help or willing to do what it takes to get better. If you are in this situation, I empathize with you. This is probably one of the scariest and most stressful situations a parent can experience. If this describes your predicament, you may have to take certain actions that your child won't like.

The least restrictive option in this case is potentially family therapy. Sometimes parents are unintentionally doing things that "reinforce" a child's depression and facilitate the child continuing to be depressed. For example, I have worked with parents who let their child stay home from school when they were feeling sad or bought them presents to cheer them up, or who only gave positive attention when the child was "sick." As you might imagine, this dramatically increases the chances of a depression continuing. If any of these sound familiar in you or your child's other parent, you might consider a course of family therapy to change these dynamics.

If your child is depressed and refuses this book and individual therapy, and they are also severely impaired (behaviors such as refusing to go to school, isolation, self-harming, grades tanking, and/or heavy substance use), you may need to do a "higher level of care." This can include Intensive Outpatient Programs (IOP) and Partial Hospitalization Programs (PHP). If your child is dependent on alcohol or drugs, they may need a Rehabilitation Facility (Rehab) or a Wilderness Program. If they are imminently suicidal or have attempted suicide, they may need a short stay in a psychiatric hospital for assessment and stabilization. If you find yourself debating amongst the above choices, and you live in the Bay Area, I just came across a fantastic resource that may be of help to you. It is called *Suicide Risk in the Bay Area* by Eli Merritt, MD. This book succinctly explains the differences between "levels of care" in psychiatry and has very practical details like names of programs and their phone numbers. I also found the sections on "how to talk to your teenager about suicidal thoughts" to be specific and helpful.

My hope is that it will never come to the above choices. There is a very reasonable chance that following this book carefully may be all that is needed, particularly if depression is caught and addressed early. If that is insufficient, a short course of Cognitive Behavioral or TEAM Therapy may be best, and there is no shame in getting additional help. I believe that if you follow all the recommendations in this chapter, your child has the best chance of recovery. The fact that you have invested enough time and energy to purchase and read this book already shows that you care tremendously about your child. I hope that this book may be part of a successful and rewarding recovery.

Sleep

I have been nervous about writing this particular chapter, because I'm worried that it will be so boring, it will put you to sleep. Or that I'll be so bored writing it, I'll fall asleep myself. You might have cringed just seeing the title of this chapter, "Sleep."

So, you might ask, if this topic is potentially so dull, why discuss it at all? Good question. I think it's somewhat ironic that this is the first chapter I'm writing in a coffee shop, where numerous customers drink the most popular drug in the world, caffeine, in part to ward off the effects of fatigue.

The reason I'm giving this topic not just one, but three chapters of coverage is that depression and sleep are very connected. Scientists have increasingly discovered that sleep not only impacts our ability to learn, react quickly, perform optimally, and fight off germs, but it also has a profound effect on our mood. In fact, research shows that adolescents often have trouble sleeping long before they develop depression (Lovato & Gradisar, 2014). In a large-scale community study of over 1,500 teens, 76% of those who experienced a major depressive episode had sleep disturbances a year earlier (Lewinsohn et al., 1993).

Still, the National Sleep Foundation reported that 59% of 6th through 8th grade students and 87% of high school students sleep less than the recommended 8.5-9.5 hours during the school week (American Academy of Pediatrics, 2014). While depression can hardly be attributed solely to sleep issues, it's clear that being mindful of your sleep patterns is crucial for protecting your mental health.

You have probably already experienced how much your sleep can affect your mood, but if not, feel free to test out this hypothesis on your own. Try getting less than six hours a night of sleep for one or two nights, and then see how chipper you are when your parents ask you to take out the trash or do your math homework. My hunch is that you will be grouchier than usual.

Your performance in school will also probably suffer after so little sleep. Do you try to fit in a few extra hours of schoolwork burning the midnight oil? If so, your grades may actually drop. Research suggests that your GPA is directly related to how much you sleep. In one study, college students who slept six hours or less per night had lower GPA's than those who slept at least nine hours per night—an average 2.74 vs 3.24 (Kelly et al., 2001). So, "night owl" behavior can actually hurt your academic performance. Teenagers who tend to be more active and alert at night not only perform worse in school, they are also more depressed, less alert during the day, and have poorer sleep quality (Short et al., 2013).

To offer some perspective, sleep deprivation can produce effects quite similar to being drunk. After 17-19 hours of sleep deprivation, performance scores in grammatical reasoning, reaction time, hand-eye coordination, memory, and other basic cognitive-motor functions are equal or worse than scores received with a blood alcohol level of 0.05%—nearly above the legal limit (Williamson & Feyer, 2000)!

In my experience as an adolescent psychiatrist, I have certainly seen many cases of sleep deprivation not only impairing academic performance, but also exacerbating or even causing episodes of depression. One of the most remarkable examples of this was Anthony, a 16-year-old boy who was one of my first patients in private practice. He was bright, sarcastic, and loved Model UN and keeping up with the news. He had done very well academically throughout most of high school, but just as he was getting ready to apply to colleges, his grades started tanking and he became very irritable. He began staying in his room for most of the weekend, snapping at people, and frequently stayed up until three or four in the morning. Within a few weeks, he went from A's and B's to D's and F's, and he walked with his head hung low, mumbling to people without making eye contact.

Anthony's parents called me very concerned both about his depression and that he might be blowing his shot of getting into any colleges if this wasn't addressed quickly. He was ambivalent about getting treatment but agreed to see me for an evaluation. It became apparent pretty quickly that he was depressed. There were a number of factors in his life that could have been involved in causing his depression, including his relationship with his parents, a conflict with a friend, and a recent romantic rejection.

However, what jumped out at me the most about Anthony was that he was staying up late almost every night, now averaging about four or five hours of sleep per night on weekdays. I suspected that so little sleep was a major player in his low mood.

I told Anthony that I'd be happy to try to help him if he wanted to work with me but that he would have to be willing to work on his sleep habits, even if this was very challenging. He was again ambivalent, but he was ultimately so miserable that he was willing to make some radical changes.

We made the two major changes that I'll teach you about in the next chapter, and Anthony quickly went from sleeping four or five hours per night to eight to nine hours per night. His parents called me a week later and left a message: "It's like he's a new man. He's back to his old self. He's much less irritable, he's making jokes again, and he's even showing interest in school again. Thank you!!"

I was excited to hear this news and saw Anthony for an appointment two days later. His parents were right—he was truly different. During our initial consultation, he was looking down so often that I barely remembered what his face looked like, but that day he held his head high and even cracked some jokes. He told me he was excited about an upcoming Model UN tournament and wanted to get caught up on his schoolwork. We were both pretty amazed at how much happier he was after just focusing on his sleep.

Since that time, I've seen many other teens and young adults who improved substantially once they got adequate sleep. The results aren't always as dramatic as they were with Anthony, but getting seven or more hours of sleep per night often helps significantly with mood.

I've also found that Cognitive Behavioral Therapy doesn't work so well to treat depression when clients are chronically sleep deprived.

Even if they are trying their hardest to learn how to change their thoughts and feelings, it is incredibly challenging to feel happy when we are exhausted.

Now, don't get me wrong, I am not saying that getting enough sleep is the only thing you need to do or that if you accomplish this feat, all your problems will miraculously dissolve and you'll be in a state of euphoria for the rest of your life. I'm not that naive. However, although getting adequate sleep may not be *sufficient* to get rid of your depression, I do believe that this is a *necessary* condition if you want to improve your mood.

If you are already consistently sleeping eight or more hours per night every night, you can ignore this whole chapter. Congratulations! You are in a very small group. For most of us, myself included, getting a healthy amount of sleep is a major challenge. And, unfortunately for you, your brain and body are still growing, which means you might even require more than eight hours of sleep every night for optimal functioning—like eight to ten hours per night!

Getting nine or ten hours of sleep a night probably sounds impossible right now. We'll address that in a few minutes. The good news is that if you start sleeping a healthier amount, you will probably get some additional perks beyond just the lifting of your depression. If you follow my recommendations in the next chapter and get enough sleep, you will likely be less irritable with your friends and family. You will have better focus in school and after school, which will probably result in better grades and may mean that you'll need to spend less time on homework. You will get sick less often. You will have more energy to exercise and learn new things. You will probably also find that when life throws challenges your way, you will be better equipped to handle them without having complete meltdowns.

By now, you might be feeling motivated to improve your sleep. Either way, let's think of all the great reasons you should continue to stay up late and cheat yourself on sleep. There are some really good ones. What are some advantages you can see to staying up past 11:00? Write them down here and don't go on until you do.

1. have sex w/ less chance of intrusion /
    masturbating

2. think clearly when alone

3. __more time to self__

   _____

4. __don't feel rushed, resting time,__
   __time to eat, watch netfleix, chill etc.__

5. __Stay up late w/ homies__

   _____

6. __rewrite constitution__ and think of
   ways to abolish police and dismantle
   while supremacy + LOVE trump

If you didn't write down at least two reasons to stay up late on the previous page, please stop reading right now and go back and write down a few. Great, thanks. What did you come up with? Here is my list (with some added from my clients):

1. There are lots of great TV shows I can watch if I stay up later

2. I had a hard day, I *deserve* to stay up a little bit and unwind

3. I have a lot of homework to do so I need to stay up late to get it done

4. I have a test tomorrow. I need to stay up late to study so I'll do well

5. My parents bug me during the day. After they go to sleep is the only time I can do what I want without them bothering me, so I need to stay up late

6. I can just drink coffee and get by tomorrow on five hours of sleep. It will be the same as if I slept more, but this way I'll get more work done

7. I told my friend/boyfriend/girlfriend I would FaceTime with them at 10:30. I can't let them down, and I'm looking forward to it anyways

8. There's an awesome party tonight. It doesn't really get going until 10:00, so I need to stay out until at least midnight if I'm going to have any fun

9. There are a lot of important articles on my phone that I need to read

10. I'll just read one more article. I'm not that tired anyway, I'll go to bed soon

11. My friend just told me about this hilarious YouTube video. I need to check it out. And any similar videos that I come across afterward

12. I just need to post a few pictures on Instagram, it can't take more than a few minutes

13. Several people texted me while I was doing work, and it would be rude not to return their messages before I go to bed. I'll just send a few texts, this won't take that long

Do any of these sound familiar? I certainly struggle with some of them myself, particularly the idea that I "deserve" to stay up for a bit, and there are some really enticing distractions on screens that are hard for me to turn away from and ignore. The good news is that you can stay up as late as you want every night and sleep as little as you want. The bad news is that if you cheat yourself on sleep, you will probably stay depressed no matter what else you do. So, it's a tough choice, but it's ultimately your choice.

We live in a time and place where there is so much academic pressure, it feels nearly impossible to get homework done, play a sport or go to an activity, have dinner, and still get at least seven or eight hours of sleep every weekday. It's certainly very challenging. But, ultimately, this is a decision that you have to make. Would you rather stay up late and probably stay depressed, have less focus in school, and take longer to do things, or become more efficient, spend less time on homework and screens, sleep more, and likely feel better? It's truly a tough choice that each of us has to make every night, and I respect that it's a challenging one.

Let's do a CBA to help figure out whether or not you want to commit to getting consistent, regular sleep.

Behavior: Go to bed early enough every night to get 7-9 hours of sleep

Pros	Cons

Pros
- Feel well-rested, enough energy to do things
- improved mood
- less likely to have body aches
- brain functions better
  → less negative thoughts
  → happy thangas, happy life
- retain info better
- creative flows
- more energy to do what you want / motivated

Cons
- anxiety to please people respond to ppl
- a lot of ppl are awake at night
- miss out on alone time
- miss out on parties/events, late night adventures
- feels like time is missed out being productive for homework
- memes hit diff @ night
- late night convros romanticized

35% / 70%

65% / 30%

80

Hi. So, how did it turn out for you? One possibility is that the Cons were greater than 50%. This means that you either officially decided you would like to be chronically sleep deprived, or that every night you'd like to "play it by ear" and aim for good enough sleep, but make exceptions when you have a test or a lot of homework or a good party that you don't want to miss.

If that's the case, I support you. The advantage of that choice is that it gives you more flexibility and more time to do the things you love. I understand. The only issue is that if you make this choice, I can't help you with your depression. I can only help people who are consistently well rested and who make this a priority. I recognize that's a tall order, and it may not be for you right now. If that's the case, not a problem. Feel free to work on your depression with someone who is less attached to you being adequately rested and we can hope for the best. Or, you could try some other strategies, and if they don't work as well as you want and you get to a place where you're willing to make getting adequate sleep one of your top priorities, feel free to come back and pick up this book at that time.

My only request is that if you are not committed to getting at least seven hours of sleep every night for the next month, then please don't go on to the next chapter. It will be a waste of your time if you're only "half in." And please don't skip to future chapters. If you're not adequately rested, the other techniques won't work very well. Then you will feel frustrated that they're not working, you might feel angry with me that they didn't work very well, and I will feel annoyed that you disregarded my instructions and kept reading before you got your sleep under control. Sound fair? You can always come back if your life and/or priorities change. I'll still be here, and we can start fresh. Best of luck to you.

If, on the other hand, your Pros column came out stronger, or you are back after deciding that sleep is higher on your priority list, Welcome! There is hope that you can be much happier than you are now and feel more refreshed. I'll show you how in the next chapter. And thanks for staying awake throughout this chapter!

Cheers to being more alert and energized. Let's get to how to achieve this right now.

6

Electronics-ectomy and Three Alarms

My hope is that if you have made it this far, you are pretty motivated to improve your sleeping patterns. That's exciting news since almost all of us are irritable and short-tempered with insufficient sleep and just by rectifying this deficiency, many people feel dramatically better. My goal in this chapter is to give you some very practical specifics on how to get more sleep.

The first step in getting adequate sleep is setting up your environment effectively. Most of us can agree that the only way to be well-rested is to go to bed early enough to allow the possibility of a good night's rest. However, even if you stumble into your room eight to ten hours before your alarm goes off, that's only half the battle. The other half is creating an environment in your room that will allow you to go to bed and have a decent shot at falling asleep quickly.

In my experience working with hundreds of teenagers and young adults, by far the biggest barriers to sleep are screens. Cell phones, laptops, iPads, TVs, desktops, and tablets are the major culprits. They are alluring and difficult to resist. I am reminded of the Sirens in the Odyssey that call out to crews on ships, luring them to their demise. You have probably had the experience of intending to watch just one episode of a show on Netflix or Hulu and then finding that three hours have passed. Or seeing a Facebook notification, imagining it will only take you about 30 seconds to see what this is about, and then wondering where the last 45 minutes went. Or thinking you will just send a quick text to someone before going to bed and then finding yourself in an extended texting session that keeps you up long after you meant to hit the sack.

If any of these scenarios resonate, you are not alone. Most of us in the Western world struggle to go to bed when there are exciting, enticing messages, shows, movies, and videos calling out to us to stay awake "just a little longer." A friend of mine who works at a popular social media company down the street revealed to me that there are people whose whole job is to try to make their notifications so irresistible that people just "have to" click on them, thus generating more revenue for advertisers and the company.

Compounding the problem is that even if we manage to rip ourselves away from the screens, get ready for bed, and then lay down to slumber, many of us have a hard time falling asleep. Particularly if we were just watching a screen a few minutes before. This is because of the effect that most screens have on our melatonin secretion.

Allow me to geek out on science for a minute. For 99.9999% of our evolution, Homo sapiens lacked electric lights, and our circadian rhythm was largely set by when the sun woke us up. The pineal gland in our brain secretes a substance called melatonin that helps make us sleepy. When the sun shines on us in the morning, the light goes through the retina at the back of the eye to the suprachiasmatic nucleus in the hypothalamus, which then tells the pineal gland to stop secreting melatonin. The brain gets information indicating that it's daytime and time to wake up, so it turns off the substance making you sleepy and you become more alert and awake. Then, after the sun has set, the pineal gland resumes secreting melatonin, which makes you drowsy enough that you fall asleep.

This was all well and good for millions of years before the invention and dissemination of screens. But now that we have bright, shiny LCD and LED screens on numerous devices that also send light through the retina to the suprachiasmatic nucleus in the hypothalamus, the brain is tricked into thinking that it's daytime and once again shuts down melatonin secretion. Then you stay awake longer watching the screen, and even as your body becomes increasingly exhausted, the light from the screen essentially keeps you awake. Have you ever had the experience of being bone-tired, but somehow still staying awake through another Game of Thrones episode? The light is tricking your brain into thinking it's time to wake up, artificially altering your circadian rhythm. Ordinary light bulbs don't have this same effect.

So what happens when you try to fall asleep right after being on your phone/TV/computer? Because your pineal gland hasn't been secreting melatonin while you've been on your device, it's going to take about 30-60 minutes without that light to ramp up secretion again and get you tired enough to be able to fall asleep. There are some people who can fall asleep right after watching a screen, and that's wonderful for them. But if you are finding that it takes you a while to fall asleep after being on a screen, now you know why (in excruciating detail), and we will address how to fix this.

So, for my clients who are suffering from depression, I insist on an "electronics-ectomy." By that, I mean no electronic devices in your room after a set time at night. In order to figure out when that time is for you, I suggest that we work backwards. Let's start by asking yourself, what is the latest time in the morning that you could wake up every day for the next 30 days and still be on time for everything in your life? I would like you to budget in time to eat breakfast (yes, it's important!), meditate for 15 minutes (we will address this in a chapter very soon), shower (this will help wake you up and can also improve mood, not to mention smelliness), brush your teeth, and get dressed. Bonus points if you budget 15-60 minutes for exercising before class or work, but we can work on that later.

Once you have figured out the latest you can wake up and still have time for ALL of the above activities, count backwards ten hours. This new time is your deadline to get electronics out of your room. For example, if you need to wake up at 7:15 AM to make it on time to everything in your life, your electronics-ectomy time would be 9:15 PM. This means that when that time rolls around, you need to drop everything, gather all your electronic devices, turn them off, and bring them out of your room to some other location in your house/apartment/dorm. The farther away, the better. Feel free to keep any charging cables in that other room and charge everything you need overnight. And, in case it was unclear, this includes your cell phone, laptop, iPad, tablet, and iPod touch. Desktop computers and TVs can be heavy, so just bring the power cord for each of those (although I

87

strongly recommend not having a TV in your room at all, as the temptation can be too strong to stay up late). You can have everything back in the morning. Also, if you own a smartphone, please put it on "airplane mode" before you turn it off for the night. I will explain more in the chapter on meditation, but the important point is that if your phone is on airplane mode when you turn it on in the morning, it will be easier to start a meditation app without numerous notifications distracting you.

I recommend setting three alarms to help you with the electronics-ectomy. Set the first alarm about 20 minutes before your electronics-ectomy time, which will signal you to start winding down. Set another alarm for five minutes before the set time. When this one goes off, it's best to save any open documents, save a draft of any emails (or hit send), hit "submit" on anything that still has to be submitted that night, put your cell on airplane mode, and turn off all the other devices. Set the final alarm for your electronics-ectomy time. When it goes off, turn off your phone and carry everything to the appointed room, even if you didn't finish everything you were working on. If you live in a dorm room, you will have to improvise, but at the very least I recommend turning your phone off and putting it somewhere difficult to reach so that it's less tempting to turn on and interact with before morning.

The reason for taking all of your devices out of your room at night is that they are simply too distracting. If your phone is on and in your room, even if it's on airplane mode, if you wake up in the middle of the night, you will be tempted to turn it to regular mode and see if anyone tweeted or texted you. You may not even attempt to fall asleep until the wee hours of the morning if you have a screen in your room, because you will always be able to find "one more" video/show/article to waste precious time on instead of sleeping and having more energy for the next day.

The reason to vacate the electronics ten hours before you need to wake up is to allow 30-60 minutes for your pineal gland to go back to secreting melatonin, so that ideally you can get about nine or nine and a half hours of sleep each night. You might need a little more or less than that since everyone is different, so feel free to play around with the numbers a bit. See how many hours you need to feel well-rested in the morning after a shower but without any caffeine.

Once you have set your electronics-ectomy time, stick to it EVERY night. No exceptions. This includes the night before a test, a major project, paper, report, anything. Here is why. Let's say you start off strong sticking to 9:15, or whatever your time is, and then a night comes around when you haven't finished your homework or studying for a test by that time and you decide to extend it until you're done. That sounds reasonable on the surface, but what do you think will happen if you make an exception this time? Pretty soon, almost every night will become a night that you "just didn't get everything done" when you needed to, and you will be back to staying up late and not getting enough sleep. If you make an exception once, the system will break down and it just won't work. The key here is consistency.

Now, I think I know what you might be thinking at this point, particularly if you're in high school. "Finish my homework and studying by 9:15 every night? That's insane! It's just not possible."

I sympathize with you. Many high schools pile on homework, and when you add in things like sports, clubs, dinner, and studying, wrapping up around 9:00 or 10:00 sounds impossible. But it is possible. To some degree, you have to choose between doing all of the things you want to do as well as you want to do them and being sleep-deprived and miserable, or scaling back and being happier. This is not an easy decision. I recognize that in order to finish your schoolwork that early, it might mean giving up a sport that you enjoy. Or a club or a hobby. It will probably mean starting your homework shortly after you get home, being even more efficient than you already are, making dinner your main break, doing more schoolwork, and going to bed not long after. If you're lucky, on weeknights you might get a little time for entertainment or with a friend, but it probably won't be nearly as long as you would like.

I wish things were different in this area. I wish we all had less time allotted for work/classes/homework and more time for other things. There will come a day when you will have more choice than you do now and the potential to choose a less hectic lifestyle. In the meantime, you will have to choose between getting enough rest and hopefully being healthy and happy, or skimping on sleep, doing more things, and staying depressed. You are welcome to choose either one, but if you decide to get less than eight hours of sleep a night and you remain depressed, please don't say that it was my fault or that the book was ineffective.

For PARENTS who are reading this, I recommend figuring out with your child what time is ten hours before they need to wake up and agreeing on the "electronics-ectomy time." In the event that your child is fortunate enough to be able to get less sleep than that and still be happy and functional—and you see objective signs that their mood is good, irritability is low, and they're not tired during the day—feel free to honor that later electronics-ectomy time. However, if they try less sleep and it's not working, it's better to go back to the "ten hour before wake up" rule.

Parents, once the time has been set, I recommend letting your child pick where they want to consistently stash their electronics each night. Then, about ten minutes after the agreed upon time, feel free to walk by that area and just confirm to yourself that all the electronics are there. No need to touch base with your child about it, just confirm everything is there. If anything, you can use your judgment to positively reward them for making this difficult change.

In the event that not all of the electronics are there ten minutes after the agreed upon time, that means that your child is having trouble finishing their work on time or remembering to get rid of the electronics. The first time this happens, just remind them non-judgmentally that x time was the agreed upon time and go back to letting them get rid of the electronics on their own.

If it happens a second time (walking past the agreed upon room ten minutes after the agreed upon time and not all the electronics are there), this means that your child needs your help with the electronics-ectomy. This is not because they are bad or immoral or lazy, it's just that the draw of the electronics and/or finishing homework was very strong, and they need your help with getting enough sleep.

In this case, it would be best for you to tell them that from now on, you will be assisting them with the electronics-ectomy by coming in ten hours before their wake-up time every night and removing the electronics yourself. If there is more than one parent/caregiver in the house, you can share this onerous responsibility, or one parent can take charge and do it themselves. What is more important is consistency. Whatever is the set time, come in right then, no earlier or later, and take all the electronics (power cords in the case of TV/desktop) out of the room and bring them into your own room for the night. Do not discuss or debate this point. Tell your child that they are welcome to set a couple of alarms beforehand to remind themselves that their electronic time is wrapping up but that ultimately the electronics are leaving at the appointed time. If you make an exception for any reason, this will fail. That includes studying for a final or AP exam, working on a project, finishing a paper, etc. It is normal to get some pushback at first, but be consistent and this will die down. Then, they can have the

electronics back in the morning. If, after a month of this, your child

would like to try again being responsible for moving the electronics out

of the room, feel free to do a "trial" and see how it goes, but be ready

to resume being in charge of this if the trial doesn't succeed.

Three Alarm Clocks

The final ingredient that we will discuss in this chapter is how to wake up at the same time every morning consistently and effectively. A "zeitgeber" is any external or environmental cue that entrains or synchronizes an organism's biological rhythms to Earth's 24-hour light/dark cycle and 12-month cycle. One of the most powerful zeitgebers is our wake-up time. In fact, waking up at a consistent time every day is more important for circadian rhythms than what time you go to sleep. If you have depression, and your goal is to feel better, having a consistent wake-up time is incredibly important. It will help your body know when to feel tired, and if you get very consistent, often within a week you will feel exhausted by the time 9:00 or 10:00 rolls around and you will fall asleep quickly and be more rested when you wake.

A common issue that I hear among my teenage patients is "I just can't get out of bed in the morning." Does this apply to you? If you struggle with hitting the snooze button many times and/or getting out of bed at different times in the morning, this section is for you. If you happen to be one of those rare and fortunate souls that just "pops" out of bed in the morning at the exact same time every day, fantastic! Feel free to skip the rest of this chapter. On the other hand, if that is you, you probably aren't depressed, so you probably aren't even reading this right now.

For everyone else, I have a solution that will get you out of bed. It is extreme and dramatic. This is not for the faint of heart. If you are ambivalent about getting adequate sleep, this may not be the path for you. But if you are really committed to getting your sleep under control and willing to take it seriously, read on.

The first step is to acquire three alarm clocks that are NOT your phone. They don't have to be fancy. All you need is something that tells time and can make noise at an appointed time. Feel free to get the cheapest ones you can find at your local drug store or online. In fact, I recommend that you do this today. You have a couple of options. Option one: Put down this book right now, get on Amazon, and purchase three inexpensive alarm clocks and get "two day shipping." Then, you can come back to this chapter. Another option is to stop reading this chapter right now, head out to a drug store to purchase the alarm clocks, and consider this your major therapy homework for today. You don't even need to read anything else today.

In either case, please don't keep reading until you have purchased three alarm clocks online or in person. And your phone does not count as one of the three. You may be tempted to ignore this and think, "I don't have time to go right now, I'll go later today" or "I'll just get them tomorrow or the next day" or "I don't want to go on Amazon right now" or "He's being ridiculous to demand three alarm clocks. That's way too many. I'll just ignore him and make do with one alarm clock, that will be good enough."

You are welcome to these thoughts, but please still go get the three alarm clocks before you do any reading. This book is not designed to be a buffet from which you take what you like and leave the rest. It probably won't be effective if you do that, and then you'll still be depressed. So, stop reading right now and go get the three alarm clocks or order them online. Thanks!

Did you purchase the three alarm clocks yet? You didn't, did you? I knew it! Go get them. Otherwise, this won't work.

Welcome back. Thank you for getting the alarm clocks. Good decision. Now, write down what time you need to wake up every morning so that you will still have 15 minutes to meditate, time to shower and eat breakfast and brush your teeth, and ideally even budget 30-60 minutes to exercise. This is your "wake-up time." Write this down here:

Wake-up time: _____ AM

Now, set all three alarm clocks for that exact time (recall that you won't have your phone in your room at night because it's too easy to be distracted by it). Turn each one to the loudest setting. Now distribute them to the corners of your room such that NONE of them are reachable from the bed. Do this every single day.

In the morning, your alarm clocks will go off. The first rule is NO SNOOZING!!!! If you hit snooze, it will throw off your circadian rhythm and mess up everything, in addition to potentially making you late for things. So, no snoozing ever. The first 30 days of this are the most important to form this habit. After that, we can relax a little bit, but for the first month, be extremely consistent and don't cheat at all. After you turn off the three alarm clocks, immediately make your bed (to deter you from climbing back in) and LEAVE THE ROOM. The first one to two minutes after waking up are the most risky for getting back in bed, and if you stay awake, it will be way better for your sleep cycle. After you walk out of the room, splash some cold water on your face to wake yourself up a bit. Then, after you have read the chapter on meditation, go meditate right after the cold water splashing. Ideally, I recommend exercising right after the meditation and before the shower, but that one has some wiggle room.

If you follow the above steps, you will be able to "get out of bed," because the alarm clocks will be really loud and annoying and you won't be able to reach them from the bed. It works really well. For about 90% of you, this will be totally sufficient. I have used this with dozens of clients and the results have been amazing.

For a small number of you, you will be such heavy sleepers that you will need help from your parent(s) to wake up, in addition to the three alarm clocks. PARENTS, if your child is not out of the room within five minutes of the "wake-up time" every morning, this means they need your help. There are two levels of intervention. The first level is to walk into their room and remove all the sheets and covers from on top of your child. Carry the covers out of the room. It turns out, laying in bed without anything on top of you is not nearly as fun and relaxing as having stuff on top of you. This will be sufficient for most people. For those truly somnolent, the final intervention in addition to removing sheets and blankets is to fill a pitcher with cold water. Then pour this cold water on your child's head and body. I promise you that they will be awake at this point. It sounds cruel, but it really works. And if they are tired, they will be more motivated to go to bed earlier that night. Again, cases rarely get to this point and hopefully this won't be you, but this is your backup plan.

In the next chapter, we will cover some "Troubleshooting" in the event that you're still not sleeping soundly. However, for the great majority of teenagers and young adults, the electronics-ectomy, going to sleep around nine to ten hours before wake-up time, and the "three alarm clock method" are sufficient for getting enough sleep. I have seen cases where someone's depression went away completely within a week just by being well-rested. Sleep has very powerful effects on our mood, and I applaud you for taking steps to get enough rest, even when there are many tantalizing things calling out for our attention and energy. I hope you sleep well and feel better!

7

Sleep Hijackers

I debated putting this chapter at the end of the book. I even thought about leaving it out completely. I will explain why later. For now, let's just say that you will be better off if you don't even start this chapter until you have done the previous sleep recommendations (three alarms, electronics-ectomy, eight to ten hours of sleep per night) for at least two weeks.

If you are feeling really excited to keep reading, it's probably fine if you read the first section of this chapter even if you just started your sleep changes. My goal is to tell you about the most common things that can get in the way of a good night's sleep, so that you can reduce or eliminate them if they are getting in your way. Some of these "hijackers" are obvious and some are more insidious. If you are doing any of the sleep hijackers but sleeping like a champ and feeling well-rested, feel free to keep doing them! But if you are consistently feeling tired or low on energy, I recommend trying to get rid of as many of these as possible to help improve your sleep.

The biggest sleep hijackers are the ones we addressed

thoroughly in the previous two chapters, particularly spending too little time in bed, having a variable wake-up time, and watching screens 30-60 minutes before bedtime. The next most common villain in your sleep routine is caffeine.

Caffeine is the most popular drug in the world. Drug? What? Yes, drug. By any commonly accepted medical definition of the word "drug," caffeine fits the bill. It stimulates your central nervous system, increases your heart rate, constricts certain blood vessels, and affects your alertness. This is not to say that caffeine is simply "bad" by virtue of being a drug. There is a reason it's consumed by billions of people on Earth. Many people like feeling more alert and energized, and it can produce mild feelings of euphoria.

The only problem here from a sleep perspective is that caffeine can cause insomnia for many people. As a general rule, anything that increases alertness can also make it harder to fall asleep, particularly the closer you consume it to bedtime. It can also contribute to jitteriness and anxiety, especially at high doses or for those who are sensitive to this drug.

Again, I'm not saying that caffeine is as simple as being "bad." If you can consume it and still sleep fine and not feel anxious, I'm not here to judge. But, if you are having any trouble falling asleep, you may want to consider at the very least not having any caffeine after noon. If you cut back to a morning coffee and you're still tossing and turning, you may want to explore even cutting that out. I know how challenging that can be having gone on and off caffeine several times myself, but at some point you may have to choose between being wired and barely energized or irritable for a few days and then hopefully better rested.

The next most common sleep hijacker for teenagers and young adults is taking naps. It turns out that, in general, naps are disruptive to a healthy sleep regimen. This one is a bit counterintuitive. You might think, "Of course I should take naps when I'm tired. This will increase my total sleep time per day, so that's a good thing. And they feel nice."

The reason that naps sabotage a healthy sleep regimen is that for most people, in order to be able to fall asleep quickly at night, they need a high "sleep drive." In a regular day, without a nap, most people are moving around doing things, and throughout the day their "sleep drive" steadily increases. If you are doing all the other sleep hygiene tips correctly, by the time about 10:00 rolls around, you will be feeling pretty sleepy and will hopefully fall asleep quickly. If you take a nap before that, it will feel nice but then you will have a dramatically lower sleep drive when you go to bed that night, it will probably take you a long time to fall asleep, and overall you will wind up more tired the next day. Err on the side of no naps.

Another huge sleep hijacker is spending time in bed when you are awake during the day. This includes doing homework on your bed, listening to music on your bed, texting or Skyping on your bed, etc. The problem here is that our brains have certain associations that can be very powerful. For example, have you noticed how you associate certain songs with specific times or events in your life? These connections are powerful and difficult to change.

If you do homework or text in bed, your brain associates being in bed with "being awake." Every time you do something in bed that's not sleep, it strengthens that association. Then, when you lie down at night and want to go to sleep, your brain is a bit confused. It stays somewhat alert. It thinks, "This is the place where I stay awake." So, although you wish that it would instantly flip a switch and start sleeping, that doesn't happen.

On the other hand, if you stay out of bed except for sleep, your brain will purely associate your bed with sleep and you are much more likely to fall asleep quickly when your head hits the pillow.

Another sleep hijacker that most people wouldn't even consider is exercise. In general, I am a huge proponent of exercise (as you will see in upcoming chapters), especially for mood, anxiety, and overall physical health. A complete lack of exercise can also cause insufficient sleep drive at night and make it harder to fall asleep quickly. So, if exercise is so essential, why am I including it here on the hijacker list?

The reason is that exercise late in the day or at night can cause insomnia. Vigorous exercise releases several important hormones in your body and neurotransmitters in your brain, including adrenaline and norepinephrine. These chemicals can make you feel happier, more alert, and more energetic. This is fantastic in the morning.

At night, those same chemicals floating through your bloodstream and brain continue to make you feel alert, but they can also make you so alert that it's hard to fall asleep. Kind of like caffeine. This is a challenge since many sports teams play in the afternoon or evening. I would say that if you can get away with afternoon or evening exercise and still sleep fine, keep doing that. However, if it's taking a long time to fall asleep, you may want to consider shifting your exercise as much as possible to mornings.

The next hijacker is less popular than it used to be but is still widely consumed. Nicotine. Whether you find it in cigarettes, e-cigarettes, chew, or snuff, nicotine is a powerful drug. It has a number of effects on the human body, including increased alertness. As with caffeine and evening exercise, alertness is a double-edged sword. Although most of us like being as alert as possible for as long as possible, nicotine can make it harder to fall asleep. If you're really hooked, consider no nicotine after noon, and no one would fault you if you talk to your doctor about how to cut it out completely.

The final hijacker on our list is alcohol. In addition to potentially worsening depression, anxiety, and social anxiety, alcohol can also contribute to insomnia. Part of why this is confusing is that alcohol does make people fall asleep more quickly in general. The problem is that it disrupts REM sleep (or dream sleep), which is an important part of overall restfulness. We also consolidate learning and memories during REM sleep, so if you disrupt it, the math equation or biology factoid you learned earlier that day might never find its way to your long-term memory storage. Chronic alcohol use in particular can disrupt sleep regularly and contribute to grogginess and low energy.

Hopefully, if you defeat all of these hijackers, use the three alarm clock method, do the electronics-ectomy, and get in bed eight to ten hours before you need to wake up, you will be sleeping like a

champ. For the great majority of you, these guidelines will be sufficient.

For the small fraction of you that have tried ALL of these suggestions for

at least two weeks and are still tired, feel free to turn to the Appendix at

the back of the book to learn about other sleep issues. If you are

generally well-rested, you can skip that section.

8

Thoughts and Depression: Intro to Cognitive Therapy

You may have noticed that so far, we have been discussing several different "behavioral" changes that you can make to improve depression. Having a consistent wake up time and going to bed earlier are behaviors that you can do to improve your mood. There are numerous other behavioral strategies that help prevent and treat depression, and we will go into a few more before the book ends.

In addition to changing our behaviors to improve our mood, we can also learn how to change our thoughts. The goal of this chapter is to introduce you to ways that your thoughts affect your mood, so that you might feel motivated to learn strategies for changing your thoughts. "Cognitive Therapy" is a style of therapy that is only concerned with our interpretation of events and how we can change those thoughts in order to feel differently. The reason this is a valuable skill set is because there will be times in your life when even if you wake up early, exercise, and meditate, you will still get angry or feel sad or disappointed. There will be other times when you might feel quite guilty or ashamed about something you have done. In those situations, knowing some cognitive techniques to change your perceptions can be invaluable and the key to feeling better.

The idea that how we interpret events affects how we feel is not new. Epictetus was a Greek philosopher that lived 2000 years ago. Prior to his teachings, everyone believed that it was the events in our lives that determined our happiness from minute to minute. If you were in the agora and found a clay pot that cost less than you expected, that would "make" you happy. If your neighbor didn't smile at you one day, that would "make" you feel sad. Epictetus had a number of wise teachings, one of which was, "It is not external events themselves that cause us distress, but the way in which we think about them, our interpretation of their significance. It is our attitudes and reactions that give us trouble. We cannot choose our external circumstances, but we can always choose how we respond to them."

This is the basic premise of cognitive therapy—that there are numerous events that are beyond our control, but we DO have control over how we respond to those events and how we choose to view them. In the 1950s, Albert Ellis popularized Epictetus' ideas and expanded on them, creating what he called "Rational Emotive Therapy." Ellis was a colorful therapist. When he was working with a patient who was saying, "I should have done this" or "I shouldn't have done that," he chided them to "stop 'should'ing' all over yourself!" As you might imagine, some patients liked this and others hated it, but he was one of the first to highlight how much damage we can do by beating up on ourselves for our past actions.

Aaron Beck came along in the 1960s and developed "Cognitive Therapy." He added to Ellis' theories the idea that patients with depression often have "automatic thoughts" that are negative and that many of these thoughts contain "errors" that contribute to unrealistic and negative thinking. For example, many thoughts among depressed patients contain the error "selective abstraction," which is "focusing exclusively on the negatives of an event." So, if you went to a party and had five great conversations with people and one boring one and then had the thought, "That party was really lame," this would be giving too much weight to the one boring conversation and an example of selective abstraction.

David Burns is a psychiatrist who studied with Aaron Beck for many years at the University of Pennsylvania. He embraced many of Beck's ideas and added to the list of errors in thinking that can result in depression and called them "cognitive distortions." He also came up with many creative ways of defeating distorted thoughts and wrote about this in *Feeling Good: The New Mood Therapy*, which came out in 1980 and popularized Cognitive Behavioral Therapy. This book includes a lot of detailed strategies for emerging from a depression, and I still highly recommend it to many of my adult clients.

There are also many new, powerful models of therapy (such as Dialectical Behavior Therapy, Acceptance and Commitment Therapy, and TEAM Therapy) that center around the idea that how we think about ourselves and the people and events in our lives dramatically impacts our feelings and actions. It is also possible to change these thoughts, feelings, and actions in profound ways.

At this point, you might still be quite skeptical that it is your thoughts about events, rather than the events themselves, that determine your feelings. Allow me to try to persuade you. Let's start with a fairly simple example.

Let's pretend that you are texting with someone you like, and then you don't hear from them for about 20 minutes. Let's refer to this lack of texting as "the event." I will argue that it is not "the event" that determines your emotions and your actions, but rather your interpretation of the event.

Let's look at two examples, both starting exactly the same with "the event" of not receiving a text from this person for 20 minutes. In Example 1, imagine that you have the following set of thoughts: "They should have texted me back by now. It's been 20 minutes! They didn't even let me know if they needed to go! Maybe they're upset with me. Maybe they don't like me anymore."

Now, write down what feelings you might experience if you had all of those thoughts:

1. _____

2. _____

3. _____

4. _____

Did you write down some feelings above? I didn't think so. You wanted to "just do this one in my head." It won't work nearly as well if you don't write these things down. So, please go back and write in a few feelings before proceeding to the next page.

If you didn't write down some feelings on the previous page, please go back and do that NOW. I promise that you will get more out of this book if you interact with it by writing down your answers. I know it's tempting to do everything in your head, but please write these down.

What did you come up with? If I were the person who hadn't gotten the text back and had all of the thoughts above, I would probably feel some combination of annoyed, irritated, angry, upset, worried, disappointed, sad, and frustrated. Did you write down any of those? It makes perfect sense that if we had those thoughts and beliefs, we would then feel upset.

For Example 2, I would like to use the exact same initial event— not receiving a text from someone you like for 20 minutes. But, in this example, I want you to imagine that the only thoughts that jumped into your head were the following: "I wonder what happened to them. In general, things seemed to be going pretty well before this. I bet they had to run to class or work. Or maybe their phone died, that has definitely happened to me. I bet they are just busy right now, and I'll probably hear from them later. I'll go do something else, too."

If you had ONLY these thoughts, what feelings might you

experience? Write them down:

1. _____

2. _____

3. _____

4. _____

Don't turn the page until you have come up with at least two

feelings (and remember, not all feelings are negative, many are

positive).

If I had been thinking only the above thoughts, I would probably feel pretty calm and relaxed. I might feel slightly disappointed that the messaging was over for now but not at a very strong level. What feelings did you pick? I'm guessing that at least one or two of the feelings you picked in Example 2 were different from the ones you came up with in the first example.

My point is that even if two people experience the EXACT same event, they may feel really differently about it depending on what thoughts or interpretations they have about the event. To me, this is one of the most fascinating and profound discoveries ever made. This means that even if the external events in our lives stay the same, we can feel much happier depending on how we look at those events.

Now, before we go on, I want to clarify that I am not a "pure" cognitive therapist. By that, I mean that I am not in the camp of people that believes that the ONLY thing that determines our happiness at any given moment is our thoughts. I would argue that there is actually good evidence that there are other things that also affect our mood. For example, when many of us are hungry, or physically ill, we are more likely to be cranky or irritable, independent of what thoughts are in our minds. There are people with Seasonal Affective Disorder who feel sad

117

when the sky is gray or rainy, independent of their thoughts. And there are drugs that can temporarily affect your serotonin and/or dopamine levels, resulting in pleasure at first and potentially a crash later. I don't think anyone would seriously argue that the increase or decrease in mood in that case is purely mediated through the person's thoughts.

That said, I do believe that if we are doing healthy routines and behaviors, such as getting adequate sleep and nutrition, exercising, being cautious with substances, and having social experiences, and we are STILL unhappy or upset, the great majority of time this discontent is due to our own thoughts. This is certainly true in my own life. As a general rule, I tend to create my own suffering. I am quite fortunate that I have enough food to eat, my physical safety is not in jeopardy, and I have a roof over my head. So, when I am feeling upset or angry or sad, it is nearly always because of how I am thinking about a situation. I would love to tell you that because I do this for a living, I am perfect at changing my own thoughts and spend all of my waking minutes in a state of blissed-out euphoria, constantly happy and calm. I wish! I can be just as whiny and complainy and petty as the best of them.

What I feel fortunate to be skilled at is that after a while of feeling sorry for myself or feeling like a victim of the world, I am usually (eventually!) able to NOTICE that I am buying into some distorted thoughts and can then take some steps to change them.

I will use today for example. I spent about five minutes this morning dreading writing this chapter. I am embarrassed to admit this, but I had the following thoughts: "Poor me. I shouldn't have to write today. My day would be so much better if I could read or watch movies all day instead. This sucks. I'm tired, and writing is going to get in the way of my relaxation and fun." As you might imagine, I then felt sad, annoyed, helpless, and disappointed. These feelings were intense and lasted for several minutes.

Thankfully, being a cognitive behavioral therapist, I was able to notice that I was getting sucked into some unrealistic thinking and was able to change it. I did a couple of techniques (which I will teach you in future chapters) and instead came up with the following set of thoughts: "Actually, I am pretty fortunate that I have the luxury of writing for two hours today! There are lots of people in the world doing manual labor for 15 hours today, and this writing stuff is much easier than that. And, I still have time today to do other things I enjoy more, and I will probably enjoy the writing more than I fear. Also, I am the one who chose to write this book! If I really wanted to, I could quit at any

119

time, but I want to write this. I have the potential to help people by writing this, and I'm grateful that I have the knowledge and skills to make some people's lives better by writing this chapter." All of these thoughts felt believable. How do you think I felt after having this new set of thoughts? Write down your answer here:

1. _____

2. _____

3. _____

After changing my thoughts, I felt much more calm, happy, relaxed, and even excited to go write. What feelings did you come up with? The key point here is that it was not the event of "writing for two hours" that determined my feelings. It was my thoughts or perceptions of that event that determined my feelings.

I could list literally hundreds of examples of how our feelings hinge on our perceptions of an event. Rain, getting a C, being asked to prom, getting fired, getting promoted, breaking up with someone, getting dumped, even being diagnosed with cancer can all affect people quite differently depending on their interpretations of the event.

I'm going to try to guess what you're thinking right now: "Wait.

What? Cancer diagnosis? How could that possibly be 'good'? Now, you're going too far. Some things are just universally, inherently bad, and cancer is one of them." Was I close?

Yes, I would argue that even being diagnosed with cancer affects people in different ways depending on how they look at it. Most of us think of cancer as a terrifying, awful, painful, tragic thing. And it certainly can be that. I don't mean to make light of this, and I wouldn't wish cancer on anyone. I have known more people than I would prefer that have suffered tremendously from their own or a loved one's cancer.

However, it doesn't have to be all "bad." One of my favorite psychiatrists is Irvin Yalom, MD, who has written many excellent books and led many support groups for people diagnosed with cancer. What he found, and has written about, is that for some patients, cancer was devastating and every aspect of it was terrible and awful.

However, there were other patients for whom their cancer diagnosis was a "wake-up call." He describes patients who realized that they found their jobs unsatisfying and quit to pursue their dreams and passions with their remaining time left. Others decided to have more close and meaningful relationships with the people in their lives and let go of years or decades-long grudges with loved ones. Some patients with cancer felt that the diagnosis "put things in perspective," and they were able to not be as bothered by "the little things in life." Others felt a desire to help the world as much as possible while they still had time and to find meaning and purpose in their lives.

The point here is that a cancer diagnosis is not as simple as "good" or "bad." Nor is rain, or traffic, or class or your job or your parents or your body or anything else. Our human brains love to simplify everything and everyone down to "good" or "bad," but it is almost never that simple. And it is almost never those events or people that "cause" us to feel a certain way. It's the thoughts in our brain.

The bad news is that until the day you die, you will have many "automatic negative thoughts" that will pop into your mind. Your brain will quickly interpret an event and secrete a thought before you can do anything about it. And for at least a few seconds or minutes, you might buy into that thought as being true or real, even when it is definitely wrong.

The good news is that there are proven and effective strategies for changing our thoughts very quickly. We have to do the hard work of learning these skills for them to be effective. We have to pause in our emotional adventure, notice that we are potentially thinking about our situation in a way that is causing suffering, and decide to do something differently at that moment. And, if we are using cognitive strategies, we have to be disciplined enough to get out a pencil or pen and write down our thoughts, even though this sounds onerous, annoying, and challenging and we wish we could do all this in our head!

BUT, if you learn and practice these skills, notice that you're off-kilter, and write down your negative thoughts, I can show you how to feel profoundly better. I can show you how to not feel guilty or ashamed any more than you want to. I can show you how to stop feeling inferior and inadequate. You can learn how to feel happy even when the events around you are the same. And then you have true power.

9

Mental Trickery

Have you ever gone to a magic show? Or seen a really good one on TV or YouTube? I love magic shows. When I was younger, I got really into magic, particularly card tricks and pulling handkerchiefs out of my hand. I couldn't get enough of reading about magic and seeing it performed. Have you had the experience of seeing a trick done and thinking that it looked incredibly real? I love when that happens. Some illusions are so effective that unless we know exactly what to look for or how the trick is done, it looks as if the magician really did make the quarter disappear or read someone's mind.

In magic, the stakes are low and we don't really suffer by believing these illusions. If anything, it can be kind of fun. However, when our minds play tricks on us with negative thoughts, the stakes go up. There are some thoughts that are blatantly untrue, but our minds convince us that they are completely true. This "mental trickery" can cause us to feel inferior, sad, angry, hurt, upset, worried, and resentful. This can last for hours, days, even weeks. These illusions can plunge us into a depression. The good news is that if you know the "tricks of the trade" that the mind uses to deceive us, you can see through the illusion, and it becomes evident that the thoughts are phony.

Let's pick a real example. I worked with a young woman a couple of years ago who I will call Jamie. She was 16, struggling with tremendous anxiety, and her grades had started to drop because she was so worried that she was having trouble focusing. Her parents and sister were very successful, and she felt she needed to follow in their footsteps. She used to be a straight A student, but this semester she was getting all B's. She came to me with several different negative thoughts, including "I'm a bad student."

This thought was incredibly upsetting to Jamie. She believed it to be 100% true and as a result, felt sad, inadequate, anxious, and hopeless. One of the first things we did was to figure out in what ways this thought might be an illusion, even though it felt totally true. The first trick, or distortion, was something called "All or Nothing Thinking." In this distortion, a thought implies that something is "black and white" or "all or none," when really it might be "in between." Jamie was quickly able to see how her own thought contained this distortion. She realized that she was acting as if there were "good students" who got straight A's and "bad students" who got awful grades and that since she wasn't in the first group, she must be a "bad student." In reality, there is a lot of "gray area," and Jamie experienced some relief when she realized that she was in the great majority of students who are somewhere in between perfection and total failure.

The next version of trickery that we discussed can be called "Labeling." Labeling occurs when the brain makes a judgment or a criticism rather than more neutrally describing a behavior in specific terms. In this case, "bad" is a pretty strong label. The thought would be much less upsetting if it went something like "I am a student who is working hard and currently getting a number of B grades." Jamie saw that the second statement was much more accurate and that her brain's use of the label "bad" added a lot of suffering but was neither helpful nor correct.

There are a couple of other tricks embedded in this thought, and as we go through them soon, you may be able to see how they apply to Jamie's case. The point is that sometimes, just seeing the specific ways that the mind is deceiving us helps reveal how a thought is actually an illusion, even when it feels true. Jamie and I worked together for about four sessions, her anxiety improved tremendously, and she didn't need further treatment. I got a sweet letter from her earlier this year saying she was enjoying college and thanking me for our work together. Sometimes, just seeing the mental trickery in thoughts can reduce how true a thought feels, which can powerfully affect our emotions.

Before we go further, I would like to give credit where credit is due. As I alluded to in the chapter, "Thoughts and Depression: Intro to Cognitive Therapy," Albert Ellis began identifying some of these common mental tricks decades ago, and Aaron Beck added to the list. David Burns added some new ones and defined them in accessible language. I don't believe that I am saying anything original in this chapter at all. In fact, I debated whether to even include this chapter in the book, because this information can be found in David Burns' book *Feeling Good: The New Mood Therapy* in the sections on cognitive distortions. The only reason I am including this chapter is that if you learn how to identify the tricks in your negative thoughts, I believe this will make all the other cognitive techniques a little bit easier. Often, finding the cognitive distortions in a thought can "weaken" the thought and make it simpler to defeat when you use another cognitive strategy.

There are several other common ways that negative thoughts can deceive us. One such distortion is referred to by David Burns as

"Overgeneralization." In this one, we take one or two events that have gone poorly and use this to predict that future events will also go poorly. For example, if you ask someone to go to a dance and they say no, you might have thoughts like "No one wants to go the dance with me" or "No one will ever say yes to me." Can you see how this thinking is faulty?

If not, allow me to try to illustrate. Let's take your own life. Do you know how to ride a bicycle? If so, great! I am guessing there was a time when you did not know how to ride a bike, such as when you were three or four years old. Let's go back in time to the very first occasion you tried riding a bike. Think back to that moment. Did you hop on the bicycle and pedal a few miles flawlessly? Probably not. I bet you fell off. Me too! How about the second time you got on that bike? Did you fall that time as well? Most likely. So, let's pretend that young you was feeling discouraged at that time. Perhaps you had a thought like "I'll never be able to ride a bicycle!" or "I've fallen off every single time I've tried riding a bike, I'll always fall off!"

Would those thoughts have been accurate? Of course not. But could they have felt true to the young you? Certainly! You could have gathered all the data you had so far and noticed that 100% of your efforts to ride a bike had resulted in falling. You then came to the seemingly reasonable conclusion that it would always be this way! The thought ended up being a lie, but it could have felt very true, causing powerful feelings.

Unfortunately, our brains do this all the time. We interview for a job and when we get rejected, we think, "No one will ever hire me." Or, if you get rejected from a college, you might think, "I'll never get in anywhere." You are taking one or two data points and extrapolating about the future to predict that things will continue to go poorly. That is "Overgeneralization" in the same way that after two fallen bike rides, you might conclude that you would never be a successful bike rider. But you probably ended up learning how to ride a bike without falling off. The prediction was inaccurate, as was the reasoning. In fact, almost every time that we become good at something, it starts with not being good at it. Many of our acceptances begin with other rejections. The secret is to NOTICE that your mind is deceiving you with an overgeneralization and not buy into it.

I will call the next version of mental trickery "Focusing on the Negatives." If you read *Feeling Good: The New Mood Therapy*, you will see this concept described as two different distortions, "Mental Filter" and "Discounting the Positives." For simplicity, I will combine them into one topic since they almost always go together. In this distortion, even if something is going really well or is almost exactly how you want it, your brain "Focuses on the Negatives" and you feel upset.

Another patient I enjoyed working with was a 13-year-old girl named Selena. She had just had a break-up with a boy she had gone out with for six months. He was into skateboarding and smoking pot and was in the coolest crowd. She felt heartbroken and was extremely sad about the situation. She had thoughts like "I'll never meet someone else as amazing as him," "I can't be happy without him," and "This break-up has ruined my life." I did a lot of empathizing and then agenda setting, and eventually Selena got to a place where she wanted to decrease the sadness she was feeling and was willing to challenge her negative thoughts. One of the distortions she kept coming across was "Focusing on the Negatives." Now, to be clear, there certainly were negatives about the break-up, and I'm not trying to minimize how painful this was for her. At the same time, it was quite hard for her to see that there were also some positives in this situation. This might be hard, but can you think of any "silver linings" that there might be in Selena's break-up? Don't go on until you write down at least two.

1. _____

   _____

2. _____

   _____

Were you able to come up with a couple of positives? Here is what Selena and I came up with together:

1. She no longer needed to spend an hour or two per day watching skateboarding, which she confessed she found boring.

2. There were several guys flirting with her at school, and she now felt free to flirt back and enjoy this attention.

3. She had been spending all her time with this guy and his friends, and she missed her old friends. She was now able to reconnect with several of her BFFs.

Just realizing that she had been "Focusing on the Negatives" and ignoring the positives helped Selena feel somewhat happier. Two months later, she ended up going out with someone she liked better than the original guy, and she was surprised by how bummed she had been about the break-up and how true her negative thoughts had seemed at the time.

Gerome was another client who tended to "Focus on the Negatives." To his credit, his life had been far from easy. Gerome's father used to hit him and his younger sister in addition to drinking about 12 beers every night. When his dad left the family and moved far away when Gerome was seven, he felt both sad and relieved. Although Gerome's father eventually moved back to the area, he didn't visit Gerome or pay any child support. Gerome came to see me at age 16 and suffered from depression. He believed that his life circumstances justified his depression and didn't see any way of thinking differently about it. I could empathize with him, as his life was certainly hard, only having one parent around, wearing used clothes until they were worn, wondering if his father would ever try to see him again. Gerome had thoughts like "I deserve a better father," "I have no shot at doing well in life," "My dad messed us up," and "People at my school don't really get me because their lives are so easy."

It's not a surprise that Gerome felt sad and angry much of the time. I think his feelings were quite reasonable given the events in his life. That wasn't really the question in our therapy. The question was whether he wanted to feel differently even if the external events stayed the same and how to do so if he decided to change his thinking.

Interestingly, Gerome ended up becoming much happier, and I think I had quite little to do with it. He ended up doing a one-month service trip during the summer to Guatemala where he lived with a host family and helped build latrines for local villagers. He met children that lived in tremendous poverty, getting by on one or two dollars a day worth of food. He made friends with other teenagers, some of whom had no parents in the picture. He spent time with a boy in the village whose arm had been chopped off by a machete. He also met families that seemed quite happy even with very little material possessions, and he admired their deep connections and enjoyment of simple pleasures.

When Gerome came back from that trip, he was different. The external events in his life were just the same; Gerome's dad still didn't visit or pay child support, and his memory of his dad was colored by physical violence. But Gerome had a spring in his step that hadn't been there before. We only had another session or two after that, but he started talking about how excited he was that he had the chance to go to college. He told me he felt grateful that he had one parent who loved him and didn't abuse him. He had taken it for granted that there weren't guerillas regularly coming to his town with machine guns and machetes but now appreciated that this is the norm for many people. He stopped "Focusing on the Negatives." His mood stayed elevated, and he sent me an email months later saying he was still doing quite well.

The next set of mental trickery is one that my mind loves to engage in regularly. David Burns names this set "Jumping to Conclusions," which he then breaks down into two separate distortions, "Fortune Telling" and "Mind Reading."

"Fortune Telling" is when we predict that something is going to happen in a certain way. Sometimes when we predict things in the future, we are actually correct. For example, you may have correctly predicted that when you pulled on the doorknob this morning, the door would open. Often our guesses are right on.

However, frequently our predictions about the future are just that: predictions. "I'm going to bomb that test." "He/she won't want to go out with me." "My boss is going to yell at me." Although there is a chance that these will come true, it is also entirely possible that they will NOT come true. Don't take my word for this—test it out for yourself. Try predicting how someone in your family will act toward you tonight or exactly what grade you will get on your next quiz. I think you will find that your ability to predict the future on important events is similar to mine—poor! And believing that bad things are going to happen to you will likely just make you feel anxious and worried, independent of whether or not they come to pass.

"Mind Reading" is another form of mental trickery. We often think we know what others are thinking. "She hasn't texted me back because she's mad at me." "Very few people have 'liked' my latest post on Facebook, so everyone must think it's really lame." I remember a few years ago when I asked one of my supervisors to recommend me for a position I wanted. I didn't get a response back over email for two weeks straight. I knew that this was because she disliked me but didn't have the heart to tell me what a loser she thought I was and was still thinking of how to let me down easy.

A week later I bumped into my supervisor in the hall. I held my breath as I prepared for her to tell me how bad she thought I was and perhaps that she was offended I had even asked her for a recommendation. She then said, "Jacob, it's good to see you! I'm really sorry I haven't responded to your email yet. I've been swamped with work, and I'm way behind on replying to people. I think you would be a great chief resident. I talked to the people in charge and told them that I thought you would be a wonderful fit." Whoa!!

When we try to guess what other people are thinking, we think we are so right! But we are often quite wrong—even those of us who are trained therapists! When you examine your negative thoughts carefully, you may notice that your brain is engaging in "Mind Reading." Simply reminding yourself that your thought is just a hypothesis or guess, rather than what the other person is REALLY thinking, can be quite comforting.

I have dedicated a whole chapter to the distortion of "Should Statements." Please read that at some point to learn why these thoughts are fraudulent, as well as how to defeat them.

The unfortunate news is that no technique is perfect for every person. Frequently, you will need to use a combination of techniques in order to adequately defeat a thought and feel significantly better. Occasionally, simply "Identifying the Distortions" will be sufficient to completely destroy a thought. In other cases, this will help to "weaken" a thought before you come in to finish it off with another cognitive technique. In either case, being able to see through the "mental trickery" will help you be less bothered by negative thoughts. It will take

136

practice to get skillful at identifying these illusions, but the more you practice the better you will get. The next time your brain is plaguing you with a negative thought that is stressing you out or making you sad, try writing it down on a piece of paper and see if you can systematically go through all of the distortions above and see how they apply to that thought in particular. My hope is that the thought will lose some of its "magic" and you will see that it's just a trick, eliminating its power to affect you.

10

Exercise and Mood

The Verdict is in. The results are clear and dramatic. Exercise is helpful for depression. Over and over, in dozens of studies, regular physical movement has been shown to improve mood, often as powerfully or even more than antidepressant medications. Let's take a look at some of the research highlights.

Firstly, aerobic exercise may give therapy a run for its money. A large-scale meta-analysis of 39 studies that researched treatments for adult depression found that exercise worked just as well as Cognitive Behavioral Therapy in reducing symptoms (Mead et al., 2009). Furthermore, a study by Duke University researchers found that 16 weeks of either aerobic exercise three times per week, antidepressants, or a combination of exercise and medication were equally effective in treating depressive symptoms (Blumenthal et al., 1999). Sticking with an exercise routine also keeps depression at bay; individuals who reported exercising regularly after the end of the study were 50% less likely to be depressed when reassessed ten months later (Blumenthal et al., 1999). Subsequent research has shown that regardless of background or the kind of initial treatment received, those who exercised regularly were the least likely to relapse (Babyak et al., 2000).

Another piece of good news is that it is not just one type of exercise that can improve your mood. Studies have shown that resistance training is just as effective as a combination of strength and aerobic exercise (Doyne et al., 1987). In fact, there are numerous types of exercise that can be beneficial, particularly if you do them vigorously: running, weight lifting, elliptical, cycling, yoga, kickboxing, kayaking, cross-country skiing, spinning, aerobics, Zumba, rock climbing, rollerblading, and snowboarding, to name a few. Notice that I didn't include "walking" on the list. The only bad news here is that walking doesn't have as much evidence behind it for antidepressant properties as a lot of the more vigorous and intense forms of exercise. It can still be a nice supplement to your day, but you need other primary forms of exercise if your goal is to really make a dent in your mood.

More research is needed to determine the optimal quantity of exercise for treating depression, but existing studies have found that exercising for 30-45 minutes three times per week has positive effects, and a minimum of 90 minutes per week is needed to prevent relapse (Blumenthal et al., 1999; Babyak et al., 2000). "High-dose" exercise treatment has been associated with a remission rate of 30% 12 weeks post-treatment—almost double the 16% remission rate associated with shorter, less vigorous exercise treatment (Trivedi et al., 2011). But, you have lots of choices.

Another wonderful thing about exercise is that it can be used both acutely and preventatively. By that I mean that regular, consistent exercise (meaning roughly five or six days a week) can help to both stave off depressive episodes, as well as help you get out of a depression if you are currently in one.

Exercise is also helpful for reducing anxiety. Although this book is primarily about depression (I am thinking about writing a separate book for teens and young adults focused completely on anxiety), anxiety often goes along with depression and can worsen it, so anxiety is still a relevant topic. Regular exercise for 30-90 minutes can acutely reduce anxiety and can also help contribute to a calm mind for the rest of the day.

Furthermore, obesity is one of the largest public health problems facing Americans and those in an increasing number of nations. Obesity contributes to numerous medical problems, including diabetes, heart disease, cancer, hypertension, stroke, and sleep apnea, among many others. Sleep apnea can directly contribute to depression, and having multiple medical problems also puts you at a higher risk of depression. Therefore, reducing obesity reduces the chances of depression. Exercise is an integral component of achieving a healthy weight, which will increase your chances of not being depressed.

So, you are probably on board with the idea that regular exercise is healthier than sitting on the couch for 16 hours a day. In fact, before you even started reading this chapter, you probably knew that exercise is valuable and may have known that it can help with depression. The problem is that there is often a disconnect between "knowing" that something is "good for us" and actually doing it. Intellectual knowledge is rarely sufficient for achieving behavioral change.

My formal recommendation to you if you would like to be happier is to develop a regimen of exercise that includes vigorous movement for 30-90 minutes, five to six days per week. This regimen is likely to be a necessary and instrumental part of your long-term recovery and optimal mental health. But, ultimately, it is your choice. Millions of Americans decide to hardly ever exercise! Let's look at some good reasons not to exercise.

Let's start with three or four reasons to NOT exercise regularly. There are some excellent reasons. Please write down at least three here. Do this now before you go on.

1. _____

   _____

2. _____

   _____

3. _____

   _____

4. _____

   _____

Don't turn the page until you have written in at least three reasons above.

If you got here and haven't written in at least three answers on the previous page, go do that please! Thank you. What did you come up with? I thought back to when I was a teenager and young adult and came up with some reasons I used to think of to NOT exercise.

1. High school starts early enough, if I wake up even earlier to exercise I will be too tired

2. Sometimes, I just don't feel like exercising, and I don't like doing things I don't want to

3. Exercising is hard work

4. There is a big test/paper I need to work on, I don't have time to exercise

5. It's cold outside

6. It's hot outside

7. I don't feel like it now but maybe later I will be more in the mood to exercise, so I should wait until the mood hits me

8. I stayed up late last night, I need to grab every minute of sleep I can right now

9. I'll start this regimen tomorrow, tomorrow will be a better start day

10. I'm already doing a lot of other things, I don't need to also exercise

11. I walk enough during the day, that will be sufficient

12. I shouldn't have to exercise, my life is hard enough

13. I have a friend who hardly ever exercises, and he seems fine. I'll just do whatever he's doing and also skip the exercise.

14. I don't have a lot of time right now. It would probably be better to wait until I have a lot more free time rather than just do 30 minutes right now.

Did any of these show up on your list? Let's take a minute or two and write down ALL

the reasons you can think of to NOT exercise. I will give you a blank Cost-Benefit Analysis on the next page. For now, leave the side blank about the advantages of exercising (i.e., the CONS of skipping exercise) and only list the PROS of skipping exercise.

Behavior: Skipping vigorous exercise this week

Pros   Cons

If you have arrived here and have not listed at least FIVE things in the Pros section, please go back and write those down now. Depression is not defeated by doing fancy things in your mind. It generally requires hard work and effort, including doing things like writing down answers in this book, even when you don't feel like it.

Did you come up with some advantages of skipping exercise? There are numerous advantages. Whether you decide to exercise regularly or not, it is worthwhile to be realistic about how challenging this is and to acknowledge the powerful forces motivating us to be more sedentary.

Now, the next part will be more challenging. See if you can come up with any good reasons to actually exercise. Go back to the "Skipping vigorous exercise this week" CBA on the last page and write these reasons down in the CONS column. I'll wait here. ☺

That was hard, wasn't it? Although many of us "know" that exercise is healthy and important, it can be quite challenging to come up with a number of good reasons to do it. I find it way easier to come up with reasons on the other side!

The final step for this chapter is to utilize those spaces underneath the CBA to figure out which column is stronger and by how much. Don't pay too much attention to the number of items in each column. Instead, read over both columns right now and get a sense of which side feels stronger or more compelling. Is it 40/60 or 70/30 or something else? Don't pick 50/50, but pick any two other numbers that add up to 100 and write them down under each column.

It may have been an easy choice, or it might have been a close call. In either case, we can use this information to decide how to move forward. One possibility is that the Pros of "skipping exercise" were stronger for you. It might be that right now is not the time for you to make exercise a priority in your life. Perhaps you are feeling really overwhelmed with school or work. Maybe your depression is quite strong and exercise feels like too much effort at the moment. It could be that your life is very full and exercise sounds nice, but you just don't have time.

All of those are OK. It just means that right now it is not a priority for you to fit in regular exercise. The bad news is that if this continues, and you are depressed, you are likely to stay depressed. If you can find a way to feel better consistently and not exercise, I support you in this. That would be great and would save you a lot of time. But most patients I know don't experience this. They require ongoing, rigorous exercise in order to feel better.

The good news is that you can change your mind at any point in the future. For now, if you have decided not to exercise, I recommend putting the book away and acknowledging that at the moment, getting over your depression is NOT your top priority. Other things are a higher priority. I accept that. If that changes, come back to this chapter and we can see where things stand.

If you came out with the Cons side weighted stronger, you've decided that exercising regularly and improving your mood are your priorities. The bad news is that sticking to an exercise regimen is hard work and will require you to keep doing it even when you feel tired and unmotivated. The good news is that I will show you how to develop something sustainable and realistic in the next chapter. If you stick with it, you are likely to feel significantly happier and calmer and have a healthier life.

11

How to Exercise Effectively

Presumably, if you have come to this chapter immediately after reading the previous one, you are motivated to incorporate exercise into your life on a regular basis. If you are still ambivalent (or skipped the last chapter for some reason), you may wish to go back and reread the previous chapter and decide if you are willing to make this a commitment.

If you are already exercising at least four or five days a week, for at least 30 minutes per session, feel free to skip this chapter entirely. Congratulations! As I mentioned in the previous chapter, walking doesn't really count, but if you are doing anything else more vigorous many times per week, just keep doing that. If your motivation is waning or you are bored, feel free to continue reading this chapter.

If you are currently exercising less than five days a week on average, this chapter is for you. The first 30 days are the most important for making anything a habit. It is quite hard to adjust our daily or weekly routines. We get used to things, and change is difficult. However, if you can do something consistently for at least 30 days, often that thing becomes routine, and it is much easier to maintain a routine than to start one. So, I encourage you to be especially mindful of the next 30 days so that you are more likely to be consistent and develop exercise as a routine in your week.

The easiest method, and for many people the most effective, is to start with a personal trainer. There are two significant advantages to hiring a personal trainer. The first advantage is accountability. A trainer will expect you to show up at a certain time and be ready to work out, so if you don't show up, you will be letting that person down as well as yourself. This is often a powerful motivator to show up, which is the hardest part. The second advantage is that if you have paid someone money for a training session, you will probably want to utilize that service. Most of us don't relish feeling like we threw money out the window, so knowing that you are paying for someone's time may incentivize you to show up. For those new to physical activity, there is the added benefit that they can show you how to use machines in a gym properly and exercise in a way that is less likely to result in injury. Most people cannot afford to retain a personal trainer indefinitely, but often if you get in the habit of exercising several times a week for a month or two, you can then "taper off" a trainer and have more of those sessions be self-initiated. Again, the first month or so is the hardest, so if you can afford it, I recommend considering a trainer just to get in the routine of exercising regularly.

For many people, even a month or two of hiring a personal trainer will be too expensive. If that is the case, there are still other ways you can get the benefits of at least some accountability. For example, some clients I have worked with join a "run club" that meets once or twice a week to run together. These are frequently free. Other people sign up for a yoga/spin/Zumba/aerobics class, ideally paying for the class in advance to increase the chance of going. One of the most helpful books I ever read was Leo Babauta's *The Power of Less*. He recommends that when you start a new habit, you announce on social media what you are intending to change and then encourage your followers/friends to hold you accountable. He also recommends having one friend that you check-in with regularly about your progress so that they expect you to report how your exercise is going.

Some of my college and post-college clients love doing CrossFit, as it burns a lot of calories, has a social component, and they expect you to show up several days per week. Many of my teenage patients sign up for sports teams that expect them to show up for practice and games.

This is often low-cost and also provides a social benefit. The last recommendation I have for lower-cost exercise that still retains some accountability is having a partner that you work out with. You decide ahead of time which days and times you will exercise, and then you both stick to it. The only thing I don't like about that option is that it relies on the other person to also stay motivated which is a bit more unpredictable, but if they are consistent, this can be a viable option as well.

For those who are incredibly motivated, you can exercise by yourself. This offers the most flexibility and independence, but it is also the most risky from an accountability standpoint. I recommend that you try this option for one or more days per week and see how it goes, but if you notice that you are not exercising consistently when you try it on your own, spend more days per week using one of the above methods to increase accountability at first. Then, after a couple of months of routine, feel free to try slowly increasing your amount of independent exercise as you gradually back down on other forms. Or, if you can afford it and are enjoying exercising with other people, by all means keep doing that!

The next question you have to ask yourself is what time of day to exercise. This might vary from day to day. There are several factors to consider. If you are playing on a sports team and they practice several days per week, you will probably have no say in the practice or game times, so those days are an easy decision. However, on the days you are not going to practice or a game or if you are not on a sports team, you will need to decide what time is best for you to move your body.

Some of my patients love exercising in the afternoon, often after class or work. The advantages of this strategy are that you don't have to wake up earlier, it can provide a break from academic work if you are in school, and it might be easier to integrate into your schedule. The main concern to be cautious of if you exercise in the afternoon is that it could make it harder for you to fall asleep. Exercise releases a number of different hormones and neurotransmitters in your brain, including adrenaline and norepinephrine. These chemicals make you feel alert, energetic, and awake. This is fantastic in the morning. It is less desirable if you are lying in bed tossing and turning and wishing you could be sleeping. I recommend only doing afternoon or evening exercise if you are finding you can still fall asleep within 20 minutes naturally. If it is taking you longer than that to fall asleep or you are using sleep aids, you have probably exercised too late in the day and/or are on a stimulant that is causing you insomnia. In this case, I recommend you switch to morning exercise.

There are several reasons that I advocate you consider morning workouts if they are available to you. The first reason is that exercise can be a wonderful way to focus your mind on something that is not "negative thoughts." Have you ever had the experience of sitting down at home, worrying about things and ruminating? I certainly have. It can last for hours! And it feels terrible. Those hours are generally a complete waste of time.

If you exercise very intensely, you will have less mental space to worry about school or work or that girl or guy you like or who texted who. You will just be thinking about getting through the next 30 seconds. The reason this is particularly valuable in the morning rather than other times is that this can INTERRUPT the flow of your negative thoughts. This gives you a chance to then get out of your home and do something else with your time besides ruminating. I have worked with dozens of clients who have spent many hours sitting around worrying, so anything you do that gets you out of your apartment or house as soon as possible is generally positive, including exercise.

Another advantage of exercise in the morning is that it will give you a boost of energy. Although you may find it physically challenging to get through your run or workout or class, the odds are that for a number of hours afterward you will feel more alert and awake. Depression can make people feel lethargic, foggy, and tired, so generally doing things that increase your energy will help you feel better. If you wait until the afternoon to exercise, it might be harder to get through each morning, and many of the benefits you get will only last from when you exercise until you go to bed. If you start your day out with movement, you get more hours of benefit.

Another advantage of morning exercise is that people are less likely to be demanding of your time at 6 AM than later in the day. If you get up earlier than others, you can usually do your own thing in peace and not have to worry about people asking you to do something for them at that hour.

The final reason I encourage morning exercise is that you can start your day off with a sense of accomplishment. It is no easy task to roll out of bed before or shortly after the sun has risen and go do something physical. If you manage to do this, despite all the temptations to sleep longer in your warm, cozy bed, you will probably feel proud that you have done something positive for yourself already that day. Today, for example, I woke up at 6 AM and worked out. When I left my apartment at 8, I felt that since I had already exercised, in many ways the day was already a success, regardless of what might happen throughout the rest of the day.

The people who I believe have it the hardest in doing morning exercise are high school students. I think the invention of "zero period," particularly an academic zero period starting at 8 AM, is perhaps the worst invention in human history. I find it appalling that we might expect high school students to get enough sleep, go to class all day, do many hours of homework, do enough sports and activities to get into competitive colleges, and then still somehow be ready to start school at 8 AM. This is ludicrous. I think even 9 AM is pushing it, but I have little say in these matters. At the very least, I am sympathetic to how challenging it can be for you to get in regular exercise, particularly anything approaching morning exercise.

If you are a high school student and are really industrious, you may want to consider going to bed insanely early (like 9 PM early). You could get used to then waking up around 5:45-6:00 and squeezing in meditation, breakfast, and about 30 minutes of exercise before classes start. I have had some clients do this with good success. I also recognize that this is a lot to ask, and if it's too much for you, I will cut you some slack. If you can do a sport or some other form of exercise after school and it doesn't cause you to toss and turn for too long, this might be the best option for you.

For everyone else, you might have more say in when your morning duties commence. If you are a college student, I recommend not starting classes before 9 AM (or 10) so that you can have enough time to meditate and exercise before class. If you have a job, and you have any say in the hours, try to start at 9 or later. This might sound extreme, but if you have a job that starts earlier than 9 AM and you are not absolutely loving it, consider switching to a different job. On average, if you are maintaining healthy habits, including morning meditation and exercise, you will probably be happier than if you start work ridiculously early and are off-kilter from the beginning of your day.

It is preferable to start small and have some successes rather than go big and burn out after a week. If you haven't seen the inside of a gym or worn running shoes in several years, don't start with 90 minutes a day, six days a week. It will be too intense. If you are out of shape, start with about two days a week for a few weeks. If you can afford one, get a personal trainer to show you the basics and hold you accountable. Get up early enough so you can see them at 6:30 or 7 AM or something like that. Start with 30 minute workouts or even shorter. Anything you are doing that is active is better than being sedentary.

If you currently exercise sporadically but are willing to make this more consistent, you might aim for anywhere from 30 to 60 minutes of exercise, three days a week. For the first month, you might hire a trainer one or two days a week and then exercise on your own or with a class one or two days a week. Focus on slowly increasing the number of days per week. It is way better to slowly go from three days a week for a month to four days a week for a month to five days a week than to up your exercise more quickly but not sustain it.

If you are already working out three or four days a week, fantastic. See if you can just go up a little bit, closer to five or six days a week. Variety is the spice of life, so if you are currently a little bored with your regimen, feel free to add in something new. You could try a kickboxing class or a new type of yoga. You could try challenging yourself to set a Personal Record with your mile time.

And if you are already exercising at least five days a week, congratulations! This is quite an accomplishment. Whatever your current level of fitness, you will probably find that consistently moving your body will help your mood in addition to aiding your physical health. Start slow and be gentle with yourself. There will be numerous things to tempt you away from exercising on any given day, but if you make yourself do it, I think you will find many benefits over time.

Remember, the first 30 days are the most important for making something a habit. Just focus on getting through the next 30 days, and then the rest will take care of itself. You can do it!

12

"Should" Statements and Entitled Thinking

I'm going to make a bold claim. This only applies to those who have a roof over their head and reliable access to food and water. But if you fall into this category, I assert that about 95% of the suffering that you experience at any given time is due to "should statements." Your suffering is not due to traffic or your job or the weather or your family members. Your suffering is due to should statements. I will show you why I think this is true and how to reduce this suffering tremendously.

Should statements take many forms. Many of these statements are about people and the world around us. "My teachers should give less homework." "My parents should leave me alone." "My sibling should be less annoying." "I should have a nicer car." Other should statements are about ourselves or our behaviors. "I should be smarter than I am." "I shouldn't be so lazy." "I should have clearer skin." "I shouldn't have sent that text yesterday."

There are many problems with should statements, but the most important one is that every time we buy into a should statement about ourselves or others or the world, we experience negative emotions. We feel some combination of anger, disappointment, frustration, resentment, or sadness. Every time. Don't take my word for this. Try this out now for yourself.

First, let's get a baseline for you right now. Imagine that for any given emotion or feeling, you can experience it anywhere between 0 and 100%. 100% means that this is the absolute strongest, most intense version of that feeling you could ever experience. 0% means "not at all." At this very moment, how strong are the following emotions for you between 0 and 100%? Write down your answers now:

Anger: _____%

Resentment: _____%

Disappointment: _____%

Frustration: _____%

Sadness: _____%

Please don't go on to the next page until you have written in numbers above.

Write down a few should statements that feel true to you right now. They can be about yourself, others, the world, or a combination.

1. _____

   _____

2. _____

   _____

3. _____

   _____

4. _____

   _____

Now, let's retest how you are feeling. Don't look back on the previous page, just close your eyes and think about each emotion and how strong it is for you at this exact moment. Write the answers down below.

Anger: _____%

Resentment: _____%

Disappointment: _____%

Frustration: _____%

Sadness: _____%

For each emotion, compare the "before" and "after" scores. What most people find is that they feel more upset after thinking about should statements than before. This is a problem, particularly given the fact that most of us have many should statements go through our mind on any given day.

In general, the more intensely we believe a should statement, and the more we are bothered by it, the more upset we will be. The problem is almost never how the world actually is in this very moment. The problem is that we are not accepting the world as it is or ourselves as we are. We are demanding that reality be different than it is. Then, we suffer.

One of my favorite patients is a young man named Karl. Karl went to Harvard for undergrad, then got a Masters at Yale, then had a very successful several years at Microsoft. He did so well there that he was able to quit, and working became optional for a while. He became a skilled yacht racer and won races in downhill skiing. He has many friends and a wonderful girlfriend, he vacations in Aspen and Fiji, and he started a company that is showing promise.

On the surface, Karl has the perfect life. Yet he struggles with low self-esteem, and this has impacted his mood significantly. He often has thoughts like "I should be more successful," "I should be smarter," and "I haven't achieved enough."

What's your diagnosis? Is the problem here that Karl isn't smart enough? Is the problem that he needs to achieve more? Do you think that if he wins one more award or his company becomes more successful, then he will be happy? No!! Karl is one of the brightest and most accomplished clients I have worked with, and it was hard for me to see him beating up on himself and feeling so inadequate.

The problem is his should statements and his thinking. My task with Karl is helping him learn to accept himself as he is, rather than demand that he be "better" or different than he already is. Most of us are actually more similar to Karl than we are dissimilar. The problem is not that we are inadequate or lazy or stupid. The problem is that we set up very high expectations of ourselves and the world, and then we are disappointed.

You might be thinking to yourself right now, "Well, I'm not like Karl. My life sucks. My problem is not 'should statements,' it's that my life is terrible and it's not going to get any better. I don't have any yachts or money, and I'm tired of hearing about your rich patients with easy lives. You don't get me." Am I close?

Let me tell you about Gina. Gina's mom has bipolar disorder and denies that there is anything going on. Her mom goes into unpredictable mood swings and screams at her for no reason. Gina also has a medical condition that makes her deaf in one ear, she can never get on a plane for the rest of her life, and if she drives somewhere where the altitude changes too quickly, it could burst the other ear drum and she would be completely deaf. Gina never met her father, and she works after school and on weekends to help her mom make rent. She also was figuring out whether she identified as "lesbian" or "bisexual," but she knew she didn't feel accepted by her current friends.

When Gina came to see me, she had been miserable for the past year. As you might imagine, she had a lot of "should statements." "I shouldn't have a medical condition." "My mom should get her own help." "I shouldn't have to work so hard." "I deserve to have two parents around." These should statements contributed significantly to her depression.

I did a lot of empathizing with Gina. I also wish that she had a better life and know that she's had to work really hard for what she's got. No question. We eventually did a Cost-Benefit Analysis of holding on to these should statements and her depression, and she decided that it wasn't worth it to keep feeling this way. We used several of the techniques that I will describe next, and within a month, Gina was feeling significantly better. The amazing thing was that her mom was the same, her financial and medical situation was the same, but her attitude toward life changed. She became significantly happier, her quick wit came out again, she ended up becoming very involved with an LGBTQ group at her school, and she made several friends who accepted and valued her. She texted me excitedly last week that she got into her top choice college! Let's take a look at how Gina turned things around.

One caveat with my diatribe on should statements is that there are frequently two significant advantages to believing them. The first is that holding on to a should statement at a strong level shows that we have high standards. When we believe that "I should study more," it shows that we have high standards for our work ethic. When we believe that "there should not be war in the world," it shows that we care about peace, and our outrage is a testimony to our high standards for how the world should be. Many of us are proud of our high standards and are reluctant to lower them.

The other advantage of should statements, in general, is that they can sometimes motivate us to change our behavior. I am currently working with a 20-year-old man named Jose. Jose is living with his parents and going to a local community college. He has several things he struggles with, including procrastination. For example, Jose didn't return his library books for a couple of years and racked up hundreds of dollars in fines. He delayed registering for classes for weeks and then received less desirable classes. When he finished eating his lunch while watching TV, he would frequently slide his crumb-filled plate under the couch, expecting to put it in the dishwasher later. He almost always forgot, and when his parents would find the plates days later, it drove them crazy.

When Jose came to see me, he had thoughts like "I shouldn't procrastinate so much," "I should get things done on time," and "I should take my plate directly to the dishwasher when I'm done."

Do you think that I told Jose, "These are just cognitive distortions! All we need to do is get you comfortable with your behaviors. Keep racking up library debt. Keep leaving dishes under the couch. Let's just help you feel good about yourself"?

No way! I agreed with Jose. His behaviors were causing him

169

trouble and making his life a lot harder. And the should statements were a sign that he wanted to change his behaviors in a positive direction. So, we worked on some skills for how to procrastinate less and get things done faster. He became more responsible and now has higher self-esteem as a result.

The point here is that there are occasional times when we DO need to listen to our should statements. They can motivate us to change our behavior in ways that might benefit us and the world, and listening to them can be a fantastic motivation to improve our lives.

That said, there are numerous things about ourselves and the world that we have no control over. In those circumstances, buying into should statements brings no obvious benefit but does cause us to feel upset consistently. "I should be taller." "I should be more coordinated." "This line should be moving more quickly." "My mom should be less annoying."

In these situations, particularly when we believe that other people should be different than they are or the world should be different than it is, we are using "Entitled Thinking." This was one of the strategies Gina ended up using frequently. You may not like what I have to say here. It is fairly extreme. However, if you accept this notion, even when it is challenging, you may feel significantly happier.

I'm going to assert that you are entitled to NOTHING. The universe owes you nothing. The universe owes me nothing. You don't deserve for anything to happen a particular way. I don't, either. In fact, none of us even "deserve" to be alive right now. The whole concept of "deserving" is both ludicrous and unhelpful. Let's pretend that I believe the thought "I deserve to live forever." What does that even mean? Does that mean that if I don't get this demand, something has gone haywire? Is there someone I can appeal to for justice on this matter? If I write a letter to the complaints board, will I then be able to live forever? No! Not only do I not deserve to live forever, I choose to believe that I don't "deserve" anything. The universe doesn't owe me a damn thing.

Any time that you buy into a should statement, you are engaging in "Entitled Thinking." Let's pretend that you go to the grocery store and the shortest line is a ten-minute wait, and you think, "I shouldn't have to wait in such a long line. I deserve to have shorter lines." I don't want to be mean or insensitive, but when you believe that, you are actually being Entitled. You are asserting to the world that you "deserve" something better. Where is the evidence for this? Is there a rulebook that contains the rule "No one should ever have to wait more than five minutes in line for something"? No, there is no such rule. Nor is there a rule that "People must act kindly and compassionately." Or a rule that "School should always be the way that you want it" or "Your parents should always be perfect." I wish that such rules existed and the universe bent to our every whim and desire, but that's not how it works. It will never work that way.

And believing these statements is completely unhelpful, because if you buy into "Entitled Thinking," you will constantly feel disappointed and upset. You will feel and act as if you have been cheated by the world. You haven't been. The harsh truth is that the world owes you and I nothing. This is sad but true. The sky rains whether you want it to or not, insects don't care if you want their bite, and most world rulers don't care about your political beliefs. You will become sick and age whether you want this or not. It has always been this way and will always be this way.

To get darker for a moment, try taking the concept of "deserve" out into nature. Would you say that a fish doesn't "deserve" to get eaten by a bird? Or that an antelope doesn't "deserve" to be devoured by a lion? What does that even mean? Who will you call to rectify this situation? This is just the way things are. "Deserve" doesn't enter into it.

There is a tremendous amount of chance in the world. I have seen generous, loving people get cancer at young ages and die, and I have seen cruel people get lucky breaks. There is much randomness and unpredictability in the way the world works.

To get a bit more extreme, I believe that none of us even deserved to have been born. It could easily have been otherwise! Imagine for a moment that your parents had never met. You would never have even existed and experienced a single minute of joy. You could have been born at a time when the Plague killed young children. You could have been born blind or deaf. You could have been born paralyzed or with missing limbs.

The above paragraphs might sound morbid or absurd. Maybe you think I'm being overly dark or pessimistic. What you might find strange is that when I think about all the awful things that could have happened to me, I actually feel happier. I like believing that I don't "deserve" anything. Because then, everything good or positive that happens feels like a "bonus."

The paradox here is that when you let go of demanding that the world or your parents or anything at all "owes" you anything, you become freer. Lighter. Anything positive that happens becomes an unexpected gift. Think of the last time that something good happened to you out of the blue. A compliment someone gave you. A better grade than you expected. Work ending early. How did you feel when these things happened?

Most of us feel excited or pleasantly surprised when something good happens out of the blue. It is actually possible to have this experience much more frequently. The next time that you go to an event or face an experience, try approaching it with the following mindset: "I have no idea how this will turn out. I have no idea if it will be enjoyable or not. It might be terrible the whole time. I don't deserve for it to be any particular way." See how this goes.

What I have found, and my clients have found, is that when we approach a situation with expectations that it will be wonderful or amazing or even "good," we frequently get disappointed. Movies let us down, classes let us down, jobs, friends, everything. We feel cheated and that this was somehow "unfair."

In contrast, if you can manage to approach a situation with very low expectations, you might be pleasantly surprised. You certainly won't feel disappointed. If you can go through the world believing that you don't deserve anything, it is incredible how many "bonuses" you might experience on a daily basis. If you don't expect anything of your walk to your car or school or job, and then you notice a beautiful flower that also smells lovely, you might be happy that you experienced this moment of joy. If you expect nothing of people around you, and they say something funny or kind, you might feel excited.

I confess, it is not at all easy to lower your expectations! As a friend of mine is fond of saying, "Going into a party with no expectations is akin to enlightenment." There is truth to this. But if you can at least recognize that your expectations are causing your suffering, this is the first step. And anything you do that lowers your expectations is likely to lead to more happiness.

The opposite of "Entitled Thinking" is "Grateful Thinking." Gratitude is so important that I will devote a whole chapter to this topic, but in short, if you focus on how wonderful it is that you have legs that can move or eyes that can see or a consistent roof over your head, you are much more likely to feel happy than if you focus on what you don't have.

Therefore, one technique that you can do when you find yourself suffering from a should statement is to switch to focusing on gratitude. For example, if you have the thought "I shouldn't have so much history homework," you could instead try to reframe this thought into something that also feels true but looks at another aspect of this situation. You might come up with "Although I have a decent amount of history homework tonight, I don't have too much math homework right now." Or, "Although I have a lot of history homework, there are many teenagers in Africa that don't have access to any school at all. They have almost no chance of going to college, and some of them probably wish that they could attend any school. I am fortunate to have access to an education."

The last technique that you can use with any should statement is one I learned from David Burns that he describes well in *Feeling Good: The New Mood Therapy*. It is called the "semantic technique." The idea behind it is that language is important, and the words we choose for our thoughts can dramatically impact how we feel.

When we say that something "should" be a certain way, we are clinging to an outcome—we are demanding that reality be exactly the way we want reality to be. The Buddhists have been saying for thousands of years that clinging (which is essentially the same as should statements) is the source of all suffering, and I think they have nailed it.

In contrast to clinging, it is completely OK to have

"preferences." For example, I generally prefer the weather to be sunny rather than rainy, and that is fine. The goal of the semantic technique is to change a thought from a demanding, clinging thought to one that is softer and more of a preference. To do the semantic technique, you replace the phrase "should" with "I would prefer" or "I wish" or "It would be nice if." For example, if I am walking to my car and I think, "It shouldn't be raining right now," then I will probably feel angry and disappointed. If I use the semantic technique, I would replace that thought with "I wish that it wasn't raining right now" or "It would be nice if it wasn't raining right now." This provides a different experience, even though the words are similar. When I instead think "I wish..." or "It would be nice if...," I don't feel as bothered or upset.

Feel free to try this for yourself. The next time you are upset about something, see if there is a should statement in your mind, like "This shouldn't be happening right now" or "This person should be acting differently." Write down whatever the thought is on a piece of paper. Then, write down a few emotions on the same paper and rate how strong they are from 0 to 100%. It might look like this:

Anger: _____%

Resentment: _____%

Disappointment: _____%

Frustration: _____%

Sadness: _____%

Then, try using the semantic technique. Replace the "should" with "I would prefer" or "I wish" or "It would be nice if." Repeat that new thought to yourself a couple of times and sit with it for a minute. Then, rescore yourself on the different emotions and see if the numbers stay the same or change.

What many of my clients find is that just this subtle change in language can affect how they feel about a situation. Try it for yourself and see if it makes a difference.

To review, most of our suffering comes from should statements, which are a form of "Entitled Thinking." The first step is to recognize that you are engaging in "Entitled Thinking" and decide if you want to stay bothered or be less bothered. If the should statement is motivating you to make a change that you really want to make right now, go make that change. If you don't want to change it or it's something you have little control over and you want to be less bothered, consider switching to "Gratitude Thinking." Focus on things that are going well in your life or ways things could be significantly worse than they are for you. If that is not sufficient, use the semantic technique. Likely between one or a combination of these strategies, you will experience less suffering.

13

Meditation and Mindfulness Matter!

Unless you have been living under a rock recently, you have probably at least heard the words "meditation" and "mindfulness." There are countless new articles and books about these subjects, and increasing studies are showing the benefits of meditation and mindfulness for numerous areas, including anxiety, depression, concentration, dissociation, pain, sports, creativity, calmness, relationships, and overall happiness.

Let's start with defining what I mean when I use these terms. At its simplest, sitting meditation is a practice in which a person sits quietly, intends to focus on something (such as the breath, a candle, or a visualization), gently notices when the mind wanders, and redirects their attention back to what they are trying to focus on.

Mindfulness has some similarities to meditation but is something different. Mindfulness is also a practice, but in some ways it is more of an attitude or an approach to doing anything that you might do in a typical day. To do an activity "mindfully" means to be completely present in the here and now, doing one thing at a time, participating fully, and with minimal judgment. For example, having a conversation with a friend mindfully would mean only focusing on the conversation at that time, not texting or zoning out, and not judging what's happening.

Both of these sound simple, and they are in a way, but neither of them is easy. By default, our minds are like wild monkeys, rushing around and grabbing at anything that comes along, rarely staying still for more than a few seconds. This might be great if our minds "zoned out" to tropical beaches or snow-covered mountains, but usually when our minds wander, they go to negative things, such as worries about the future, making plans, or regrets about the past.

The bad news is that if we don't deliberately train our minds, they can stay unruly our whole lives, leading to difficulty concentrating, anxiety, procrastination, and depression. The good news is that the brain is very plastic, particularly the teenage and young adult brain, and if you put in a few minutes every morning "training your brain" to focus on what you want it to, your mind can change significantly. Practiced meditators are better able to direct their attention to where they want it. Procrastination has also been linked to less frequent practice of mindfulness-promoting activities, such as meditation and yoga, and low mindfulness is thought to contribute to the stress we experience when we procrastinate (Sirois & Tosti, 2012).

Meditation and mindfulness have also proven helpful for those who suffer from mood disorders and physical disease. In a review of the 47 most rigorous randomized clinical trials looking at the effects of meditation on physical and mental health to date, it was found that meditation programs can moderately reduce symptoms of anxiety, depression, and physical pain (Goyal et al., 2014). Mindfulness-Based Cognitive Therapy (MBCT) has also been shown to prevent the relapse of depression symptoms, especially among those who have experienced several depressive episodes in the past. Multiple studies found that among people who had experienced at least three episodes of depression, adding MBCT to their existing treatment reduced the recurrence of depressive episodes by half over a five-month follow-up period (Ma & Teasdale, 2004; Morgan, 2003).

Let's go over how and why meditation works. In the meditation that I teach my clients (and do myself), the practice is fairly simple. I sit down somewhere relatively quiet, I set a timer or use an app that keeps track of the time, and then I pay attention to the feeling in my belly as my breath comes in and out of my body. Then my mind wanders. A lot!

My mind often wanders dozens, if not hundreds, of times in a meditation session. This is totally normal. The key is that each time I notice my mind wandering, I gently (occasionally harshly, but I aim for gently) bring my mind back to focusing on my breath. Then my mind wanders again some seconds later, and then I come back to focusing on my belly expanding and contracting. Over and over again.

The reason this practice is helpful is that if you do it daily, you are training your mind to focus where you want to focus. Over and over. It's like building up a muscle. If you want to get better at curling a ten-pound weight, curling that weight over and over again will make your biceps stronger. Same principle here. Although we are all born at different points on a spectrum of ability to focus, anyone can dramatically improve their concentration by building up those abilities through daily meditation.

The Dalai Lama himself was so confident in the positive effects of meditation on the brain that he encouraged eight of his most accomplished disciples, each with between 10,000 to 50,000 hours of meditation practice, to participate in neuroimaging research at the Keck Laboratory for Functional Brain Imaging and Behavior. Neuroimaging techniques allow scientists to measure different types of brain waves, which are each associated with different types of mental activity. One type of brain wave that is particularly relevant to meditation research is the "gamma wave." The Keck Laboratory research showed that individuals who had been trained in meditation for one week showed only slight increases in gamma wave activity while meditating. However, the Dalai Lama's disciples showed gamma wave activity more powerful and more coordinated than had been recorded in previous neuroscience literature. The monks also showed higher baseline gamma wave activity when not actively meditating, suggesting that consistent meditation contributed to permanent brain changes (Lutz et al., 2004). These and other similar findings are significant because neuroscientists believe that synchronized, high-amplitude gamma wave activity allows brain cells to effectively communicate with one another and function more efficiently (Liou, 2010).

What's more is that the monks' exceptional gamma wave activity was concentrated in the left prefrontal cortex, which is an area of the brain associated with optimism and resilience and that shows higher activity when people feel happy (Lane et al., 1997). It is therefore not surprising that steady meditation practice has been shown not only to improve mental focus and flexibility, but also to promote happiness.

The French geneticist-turned-monk, Matthieu Ricard, was recently deemed the "Happiest Man Alive" following fMRI brain scans in which his gamma wave activity exceeded any previously observed. Ricard credits his emotional well-being to meditation, describing happiness as a skill to be cultivated through persistence over time, rather than a state of mind to be chased (Barnes, 2011).

Dedicating one's life to meditation is not possible for most of us, but one need not be a monk to experience positive outcomes from a daily meditation practice. In one of many similar studies, adults randomly assigned to practice loving-kindness meditation for about 80 minutes per week for two months reported marked increases in their daily experience of positive emotions (such as joy, awe, and contentment), accompanied by increased mindfulness, social support, sense of purpose, and other personal resources, as well as greater life satisfaction and reduced symptoms of depression (Fredrickson et al., 2008).

It turns out that the practice of taming the "monkey mind" through meditation can have even more profound benefits for how we relate to ourselves and to the broader world around us. Recently, multiple studies have shown that those who meditate behave more

185

compassionately towards others compared to those who do not

meditate. In one particularly clever study designed to test altruistic

behavior (that has since been replicated: Lim et al., 2015), individuals

who completed a three-week meditation program and those who did

not sat in a waiting room where an actor pretended to be injured and

audibly in pain. Half of the meditators offered the ailing individual their

seat, while only 16% of the non-meditators behaved compassionately in

the same scenario (Condon et al., 2013). Meditation may also help us

become better emotionally attuned to those around us. In one study,

individuals assigned to a weekly meditation group that practiced

Cognitively-Based Compassion Training showed an improved ability to

accurately read others' facial expressions, as well as increased neural

activity in brain areas associated with empathy. The non-meditating

control group, by contrast, showed no such improvement in their

attunement to others' emotional expressions or increased empathy-

related brain activity (Mascaro et al., 2012). When researchers recorded

newly-trained meditators at random while going about their daily lives,

they found that they spoke with less harsh language towards others,

laughed more frequently, and used more "we" versus "I" statements

than people who had not been trained in meditation (Harris & Brady,

2011).

Our capacity to feel compassion for others—and ourselves—walks hand in hand with happiness. In fact, while individual happiness is a welcome byproduct of meditation, the primary objective of meditation in the Buddhist tradition is to cultivate compassion to facilitate the world's healing. In light of how important social connection and support is to our emotional health, it follows that practicing calming the mind and developing greater awareness of others' thoughts and feelings, as well as our own, is likely to enrich our relationships (with others and with ourselves) and give our mood a boost.

So, although this book is primarily about defeating your depression, and we will soon talk about how meditation relates to this topic, a "side effect" of daily meditation is that you might notice that it takes less effort to remember things in school or at work and your memory for things gets better, because it's easier to focus on them.

Now, let's get straight to why meditation is important when it comes to mood and depression. The first reason has to do with the "negativity bias." This concept has been well documented in clinical psychology for decades, and it's a bummer, because it turns out that when your mind wanders, in general it wanders toward negative things.

This means that if you are doing something that has the potential to be enjoyable, such as taking a walk, most of the times that your mind wanders, you will probably think about things that could go poorly in the future, or someone who is upset with you, or something negative that you did. There are exceptions, of course, but most of us, myself included, veer toward the negative by default.

This was adaptive tens of thousands of years ago when thinking about the saber-toothed tiger that might maul you could save your hide, or when worrying about what landmarks lead you to a lake could save you from dying of dehydration. But most of us in America are fortunate enough to have food and water and few animal predators. But, our brains evolved primarily to keep us alive—happiness wasn't a priority back then—so our brains still carry this negative bias and may for several thousand more years.

One of the things that is great about meditation is that if we get skillful at keeping our mind on the task that we want to focus on, it becomes much easier to enjoy that task. For example, if I haven't meditated on a particular day, and I eat my lunch, I might spend half or even all of the time thinking about negative things and hardly even notice the food I am scarfing down. On the other hand, if I have meditated that day, I am better able to focus on eating my lunch, and it is much more likely that I will pay attention to the flavors and the textures of the food. Then, this can be a very pleasurable experience and one with far less rumination. And one of the secrets to breaking out of a depression is having many pleasurable and/or meaningful experiences each day, with the goal that rumination and worrying will take up a far lower percentage of our day.

The main way that meditation relates to mindfulness is that meditation increases your ability to be mindful during the day. Anything can be done mindfully or not mindfully. You can snowboard, wash dishes, eat, and talk mindfully. And any of those can be done on "auto-pilot." You might think that when times are tough, you'd like your brain to frequently be on auto-pilot so you don't have to experience whatever is happening. It turns out, however, that zoning out is a way of avoiding whatever is actually happening and leads to more suffering rather than less.

Matt Killingsworth has a fantastic TED talk on this subject. I won't go into too much detail about it, but he describes how they gathered data on tens of thousands of people doing lots of different activities and surveyed them at random intervals about what they were doing, how much they were enjoying themselves, and how present they were at that moment.

You might think that certain activities would almost always be pleasurable (like sex or eating) and others would be terrible, such as doing homework or washing dishes. It turns out that WHAT people are doing at any given moment is less important to their happiness than how present they are during that activity. The people who were the happiest at any given moment were generally also the most present in the here and now.

This means that even when you are doing things that could be boring or repetitive, if you are able to stay in the moment and do that activity mindfully, you have the potential to be quite happy and even enjoy the activity. You may have had this experience already. Have you ever gotten into a "flow state" in which you were really engaged in something, totally absorbed in it, everything seemed to "click," and things were more effortless? I love those states.

If you meditate daily, even for a few minutes, you are training your brain to focus on one thing at a time, which makes it easier to get into flow states. It is nearly impossible to be in a flow state and also be sad or anxious at the same time. This is because you become so absorbed in the one thing you are doing, there's no space left over for worrying or even processing. This is not only quite exciting and enjoyable, but people in flow states frequently report doing things more efficiently as well as more creatively.

The final reason that meditation can have such a big effect on depression is that it can help make you less anxious. Anxiety can not only worsen depression, it can sometimes cause it. One of my favorite patients that I am currently seeing is a 16-year-old boy named Noah. He is a gifted computer programmer and piano player at Sacred Heart Preparatory and a really nice guy. Noah came to me two months ago with profound anxiety that he might become suicidal and kill himself. He had never been violent toward himself or others, but when he read about the first of eight suicides in his area this year, he became petrified that he might spontaneously become depressed and then try to hurt himself. This anxiety then dominated his life and made it hard for him to enjoy things, because he was spending so much time worrying.

We did several interventions to help Noah, but one of them was daily meditation. Within about three weeks, Noah was worrying much less about hurting himself, and when the thoughts came, he wasn't as bothered by them. He has continued to not hurt himself, feel better, and we are wrapping up treatment next week.

There are at least two ways that meditation can reduce anxiety. The first is that it prevents your brain from coming up with as many negative thoughts during the day. It allows your brain to become more comfortable with stillness and relaxation, so there are less negative thoughts that you then have to deal with.

The second way that meditation helps anxiety is that when thoughts do arise that are negative, meditation helps you be less bothered by them. Instead of identifying with the thoughts as being the same as "you," they become simply thoughts. In the same way that your salivary glands produce saliva, your brain produces thoughts. Some of those are useful and helpful, and many are just random neuron firings that aren't worth paying much attention to. I have personally (unfortunately) spent hundreds of hours of my life worrying about scenarios that never came to pass, and I would have preferred to have labeled them as "just thoughts" and gone back to whatever more enjoyable activity I was engaging in.

So, while I think there are some tremendous cognitive and behavioral techniques for defeating anxious thoughts, meditation is a powerful tool in its own right. It develops your brain's ability to not take the thoughts so seriously or personally.

This is also helpful with thoughts that can directly make you sad, like "I'm a loser" or "I'm worthless" or "No one likes me." If we buy into those thoughts, we will probably feel sad and inferior. If we instead develop the capacity to quickly say, "That's just a thought my brain produced, I don't need to pay any attention to it," then we might feel calm and happy. I'm not advocating this as the only tool for treating depression, but it can be a powerful one.

There is, in fact, a whole school of therapy now called "Mindfulness-Based Cognitive Therapy" that incorporates meditation and mindfulness into defeating and preventing depression. In my opinion, having as many tools as possible to defeat negative thoughts and be less bothered by them is wonderful. And if you can prevent many of those thoughts from surfacing in the first place, even better. Plus, being able to get into flow states frequently, resulting in happiness and creativity, can be the cherry on the ice cream sundae.

In the next chapter, we will go into exactly HOW to meditate and common myths and errors to avoid.

14

How to Meditate "Successfully"

I intend for this chapter to be short. Hopefully, at this point, you are motivated to try meditating and see how it goes. I recommend meditating for as close as you can get to every single day for at least one month before deciding if it's helpful to you or not. The easiest way is to use an app that includes a timer and some effective instructions on how to meditate. For example, I use Headspace every morning (Disclaimer: I do not at the time of this publishing have any financial ties to the company that makes Headspace, but I believe in and love this product, so I may invest in it at some point).

I highly recommend meditating in the morning. There are two reasons for this. The first is that most of us have busy lives, and once we get started with our day, it is incredibly challenging to stop and take 5-20 minutes to just focus on our breathing. By the time the day gets going, we usually feel a pressure to go fast, get things done, and it's nearly impossible to insert meditation in at this time. The other reason I think the morning is the best time for meditation is that there is a good chance you will feel calmer and more focused for the rest of the day after you meditate until you go to sleep. These effects will largely wear off by the time you wake up the next day, so I think you get the maximum benefit by meditating early in the day so that you have more time afterwards to reap its benefits.

Furthermore, I recommend meditating not just in the morning, but first thing in the morning. Building a new habit is quite challenging, and it often takes a month or more for something to become part of our daily ritual. If you are like me and are often racing to get out the door, you will probably find it challenging to stop in the middle of your morning routine and meditate. However, if you get in the habit of waking up 10-20 minutes earlier than you do currently and immediately meditate, then you will still fit everything else in and be on time.

It is much more important to meditate every day than it is to occasionally meditate for long periods of time. Even two or three minutes of daily meditation in the morning would be superior to an occasional 30-minute meditation. You will probably be surprised how even a few minutes of meditation in the morning can affect the rest of your day.

Here is what I recommend you do:

1. Read the previous chapters in this book if you have not already

done so, and use the "Three Alarm Clock Method" if you are having any trouble waking up and popping out of bed.

2. At night, set your alarm for 15 minutes earlier than you are currently waking up.

3. If you have a cell phone, turn it to "Airplane Mode" before you go to bed, and then turn off the phone (ideally charging in another room besides your bedroom).

4. Wake up, turn off your alarms, get out of your room, turn on your phone, AND LEAVE IT IN AIRPLANE MODE! This will avoid a barrage of texts, messages, and updates that could suck you in for minutes or hours and prevent meditating.

5. Splash some cold water on your face if you are groggy.

6. Walk with your phone to a quiet place nearby (inside or outside), sit down, and start your timer or the app Headspace.

7. Set an intention to try to focus on your breath. When your mind wanders, gently come back to focusing on your breath. Attempt to be forgiving toward yourself for having a wandering mind.

8. Pat yourself on the back. One of my favorite instructors in medical school introduced me to this practice, and one of his sayings was "If you sit for the whole time, you get an A. No

matter how many times your mind wanders, you still get an A."

9. Repeat every morning.

10. If after a month or more of consistent meditation you are finding benefits from the practice, feel free to experiment with longer times. But if that goal reduces your frequency of meditation, go back to less time each day until this becomes part of your daily routine.

That's it. The reason I am biased toward Headspace is that I like the prompts and how clearly Andy explains the basics of meditation. I also like the variety of different "packs" on Anxiety, Change, Appreciation, etc. If you don't have a smartphone, or don't like this app for some reason, feel free to use any kind of timer. If you have one with a gentle bell or gong at the end, that can be a bit less jarring. For years I used "Insight Meditation Timer," and I still like this app. Which app or timer you use doesn't matter that much as long as you are sitting consistently.

COMMON MYTHS ABOUT MEDITATION

1. "I am a 'bad meditator,' because my mind wanders a lot. I must

not be doing it right!"

I hear this one a lot. It turns out that if your mind wanders a lot, that doesn't mean you are a "bad meditator." It means that you are human! I have been meditating almost daily since I was in medical school in my 20's, and my mind still wanders quite frequently. That's OK. There is a reason you will hear meditation referred to as "a practice." It is because no one ever gets perfect at it. You just keep practicing. Some days your mind will wander a lot, and other days your mind will wander a bit less often. It doesn't matter. If you stick with the practice, within a few weeks (or even days) you will probably start to notice some benefits.

2. "Meditation is supposed to clear your mind. My mind never gets clear!"

This one is also a myth. Meditation has nothing to do with clearing your mind or "getting rid" of thoughts or feelings. It's not possible, certainly not for more than a few seconds or minutes at the most. But we don't need to "clear our minds." With meditation, thoughts still come and go, but we learn how to have a different relationship with those thoughts. Instead of getting as caught up with them and identifying with them, we can learn to label them as "just thoughts" and not be much more bothered by them than we would be by seeing birds flying through the sky.

3. "Meditation makes me anxious."

This is probably not the case. I suspect that if you are feeling quite anxious while you are meditating, it is not because the meditation is "making" you this way. It is revealing that you have underlying anxiety. Sitting still in silence is hard! Our brains can be relentless and at times cruel in coming up with nasty and scary thoughts about us and the world. Meditation is not making your brain come up with thoughts. It is simply allowing you to see what your mind is like right now when you pause and observe it. What I find paradoxical and amazing is that the process of observing your mind (through focusing on your breath) over time changes the mind itself. It allows the mind to slow down and allows us to give less power to the thoughts. As we learn to get some distance from the thoughts and feelings and merely label them "thoughts" or "feelings," without getting caught up in a story, over time we become less anxious.

4. "I don't need to meditate, because I do BLANK (here substitute yoga, running, or some other activity for blank)."

Here is my perspective on this topic: If you are really into running or yoga or snowboarding or dancing or anything else that you do regularly, and it has allowed you to have very low levels of anxiety and your focus is wonderful, fantastic. Keep doing that. For most of us, even regular physical activity is not sufficient to calm our minds during most of the day and identify less with thoughts. I think this one is frequently a cop-out. If you talk to experts on mindfulness, flow, and contemplative traditions, most of them will agree that while anything can be done mindfully, it is also important to have a daily sitting practice for maximal benefit.

5. "I don't have time to meditate. My life is too busy."

Sorry, I'm not going to buy this one. It's all about priorities. If you really care about your mental health and want to take this seriously, you need to carve out time. That means going to bed a few minutes earlier and waking up a few minutes earlier. Let's be honest, most of us spend at least an hour a day, if not more, doing things like watching TV, checking out Facebook, and reading articles about obscure subjects. If you cut out 15 minutes of that at night, you can go to bed earlier and still get the same quantity of sleep. Furthermore, the whole point of packing your day full of stuff is (in the long run) greater happiness. So rather than fit in more activities and hope this translates into more happiness, it is a safer bet to do less and spend more time doing things that studies show improve mood, such as meditating. I will end with one of my favorite Zen proverbs: "You should sit in meditation for 20 minutes every day. Unless you're too busy. Then you should sit for an hour."

15

Thought Detective

Have you ever had the experience of having a thought pop into your mind and it felt totally, completely true? "I definitely failed that quiz." "No one likes me." "I'm going to do terribly on this test." "I'm the stupidest person at this school." "My parents wish I was never born." Do any of these sound familiar? Thoughts like these can be quite powerful. They can cause us to feel sad, worried, upset, angry, resentful, scared, and many other emotions. But they don't have to affect us in these ways. My goal in this chapter is to show you one specific technique that can help you defeat these thoughts.

If you think back to the chapter in this book on "Cognitive Therapy," you may recall my assertion that it is almost never the events in our lives that cause us to feel a certain way, but rather our interpretations of these events. This point is worth repeating. If you don't buy into this idea, no cognitive technique in the world will help you. If you do accept it, there are several dozen strategies you can learn that will help you change your thoughts, which will change your feelings. If it has been a while since you read that chapter, or you are currently having any doubts, please go back and reread that section so that you are more prepared for the rest of this chapter.

There are two pieces of bad news you should know before we formally begin. The first is that there is little you can do to prevent a negative thought from popping into your mind. Certainly, regular meditation and throwing your attention fully into your activities can reduce how often thoughts pop into your mind, but even if you are the world's best meditator and mindfulness expert, you will still sometimes have negative thoughts that emerge from your brain. This is inevitable.

The best analogy I can come up with is to imagine you live in a place that occasionally gets some rain. Unless you walk around constantly with a hood over your head or an umbrella up even when it's not raining, it is almost inevitable that there will come a day when it's not raining at first, but you are outside and a few drops will get on you when the rain starts to fall. This is natural and totally OK. You will get a little wet. At that point, you have a few options. If you like the rain and don't mind getting pretty wet, you always have the option to just stand there and experience the rain and being wet. This is the equivalent of "accepting an emotion" or "letting emotions happen without pushing them away." This is very powerful, and to some degree, if you master this strategy you don't need anything else. For the person that welcomes being completely drenched for an indefinite amount of time, they don't even need to bother carrying an umbrella or raincoat and need not fear the rain.

For many of us, we only want a certain amount of rain falling on us. We might be able to tolerate a few minutes of being completely drenched and somewhat cold but would rather not have hours of this experience. That is OK too. After a few minutes of the rain falling, we might decide that we have had enough and walk into a building or open an umbrella. Other times, after even a drop or two we might decide to be proactive and put our hood on right away to prevent further wetness. Again, the first couple drops are inevitable, but we have some power in how long we want to experience getting wet.

If you get to a point where you want to change the feelings you are experiencing, cognitive techniques may be the next strategy to use. The goal of this book is NOT to provide a comprehensive, exhaustive list of techniques. If you still want to learn more strategies after reading this book, I highly recommend *Feeling Good: The New Mood Therapy*. The goal of this chapter will be to simply present one strategy that you might find helpful.

David Burns either invented or improved upon this technique, which goes by the name of "Examine the Evidence." This technique is quite powerful for many people. It can allow you to defeat thoughts that are untrue, sometimes dramatically changing how you are feeling. In order to do this technique, you start by writing down your feelings and thoughts on a piece of paper. Do NOT try to do this technique in your head. It won't work nearly as well. I regularly try to convince myself that "this time will be different," but when I try to do almost any of the cognitive strategies in my head to save time and effort, it fails miserably and I am disappointed. You are welcome to test this out for yourself, but at least for right now, I would like you to have the experience of seeing what it's like when you write things down.

If you don't currently have a blank piece of paper and a pen or pencil, go get one right now. I think this works better by hand, so if you are reading this on an electronic device, I still want you to go get a pen and paper. I'll wait for you. Please put this down for a minute, get the pen or pencil and blank paper, then come back. Don't read further until you have done that.

Welcome back. Did you do it? I hope so. If not, go get some paper and a pen! I'm in no hurry. OK, I'll presume you're ready. Thank you. Now, write down some of your feelings at the top of the paper and how strong they feel between 0 and 100%. You might currently be feeling sad, anxious, upset, frustrated, angry, worried, resentful, annoyed, some other emotions, or a combination. Write each one down and how strong it feels right now.

After you do that, think about what thoughts are causing you to feel that way. Remember, in almost all situations, if you are experiencing negative emotions, there are very likely thoughts that are causing these feelings. If we change the thoughts, the feelings are very likely to change, too. Write down some of your thoughts that are causing these feelings and how true each thought feels on a scale of 0 to 100%.

For those of you that are reading a paperback or hardback right now, you are also welcome to write directly in the book below if you wish. Or, you can use a blank sheet of paper. Both are fine. The only unacceptable choice is doing this in your head. Write down a minimum of two thoughts and two feelings.

Feelings:

1. _____: _____%

2. _____: _____%

3. _____: _____%

Thoughts:

1. _____: _____%

2. _____: _____%

3. _____: _____%

Thank you for writing down some thoughts and feelings. The goal of doing this is to get practice checking in with yourself, identifying your emotions at any given time, and then figuring out the thoughts that are triggering those emotions. This is a skill that gets easier with practice. Even if right now this feels very challenging, you will find that if you do this for about 10-20 minutes a day, you will quickly get dramatically better at it. Before too long, you will be able to check in with yourself and in less than a minute, figure out the feelings you are currently experiencing. Then, the thoughts will emerge as well.

Now, let's use a sample thought so that you can see how the "Examine the Evidence" technique works. Let's pretend that one of your thoughts is "I definitely failed that quiz." Imagine that yesterday you took a math quiz, and right now you believe this thought to be true 95%. Let's also imagine that you usually get B's in math and that you spent some time studying for this quiz. Imagine that you have gotten a range of grades on math quizzes in the past, but you have only failed one in your life.

To do "Examine the Evidence," you are going to imagine that you are a detective for the next ten minutes. Pretend that you are not you, instead you are a professional detective who was hired independently to figure out whether a particular thought is true or not true. Just like a detective in real life, you are not going to let feelings factor in too much, instead you are going to "examine the evidence" in the case and try to come to an objective determination. I recognize this is a little corny, but play along. Just as you would if you were figuring out whether or not someone was the killer in a murder case, you will look at the objective data and facts and use this to guide your decision.

We will use the worksheet on the following page. I will include a blank one at the end of the book, so you are welcome to write in the one right here, and then you can make photocopies of the other one if you wish. At the top, write in the thought you are examining. Just pick one. For this example, we will go with "I definitely failed that quiz."

For the next part, you will become the Detective. Again, definitely corny, but try to really imagine that you were hired by someone to independently investigate whether or not a particular thought is true. You will use your own life, history, and skills as the "Evidence," but will write this part as an independent person. Start by writing down all the "Evidence For" the thought being true in the left-hand column. Think hard. Only after you have finished that side, then brainstorm all of the "Evidence Against" that thought being true.

Before you turn to the next page, let's do a warm up. Just come up with one piece of Evidence that this thought is true ("I failed that quiz"), and write that down here:

Evidence For "I failed that quiz":

1. _____

_____

Now, do the same and think of at least one piece of data that suggests you did NOT fail that quiz. Write that below:

Evidence Against "I failed that quiz":

1. _____

_____

Then, use the "Examine the Evidence" worksheet on the next page and see if you can come up with at least two pieces of data to suggest that this thought is true and at least three pieces of data to suggest that the thought is NOT true. Do this now.

Finally, after you have come up with all the "Evidence," try to objectively assess which side is stronger. Independent of the number of items you came up with, one side will probably feel more compelling than the other. Come up with two numbers that add up to 100 that represent how strong each side feels, and write those numbers down in the boxes at the bottom. For example, if the "Evidence Against" was much stronger, you might come up with 20 under "Evidence For" and 80 under "Evidence Against."

EXAMINE THE EVIDENCE

Thought: ___"I definitely failed that quiz."___

Evidence For	Evidence Against
1.	1.
2.	2.
3.	3.
4.	4.

Don't keep reading unless you have filled out the above chart.
Did you do it? Great! What pieces of evidence did you come up with?
Here are a few that I thought of. Under the "Evidence For" column, it
might look something like this:

1. I did fail one math quiz in my life, so it's possible I could fail
   another such as the one yesterday.
2. I felt like I failed it, and occasionally how I felt about a quiz
   reflects how I actually did.
3. Some people do fail math quizzes.
4. There were some questions I didn't feel confident about, and I
   may have gotten them wrong.

Under the "Evidence Against" column, here is what I came up
with:

1. There have been multiple times when I thought I failed
   something, but I didn't actually fail.
2. I have only failed one math quiz before, so I have a pretty strong
   track record of getting C's or better on these quizzes. I probably

got at least a C on this one too.

3. I did study some for this quiz, probably enough to not fail.

4. There were some questions I felt reasonably confident about, so I probably at least passed.

Your columns may have looked similar to these or different. How did the numbers come out? Hopefully, if you only failed one math quiz in your life and you imagine you studied for the one yesterday, the "Evidence Against" column came out stronger. Did it? How did it feel to look at the data objectively rather than to just rely on your gut feelings? I like this technique because it encourages me to be more rational, and this often helps defeat thoughts more effectively.

It's possible this technique won't work for you in every given instance. If that happens, just move on to another cognitive or behavioral strategy until you find one that DOES work. And if this one helps defeat a thought or weaken it, great!

In general, the thoughts that lend themselves best to this particular technique are ones that we suspect on some level are not really true. For example, if you have at least two friends in the world, you may still occasionally have the thought "No one likes me,"

214

especially if one of your friends is mad at you. However, if you look at the evidence objectively, you will hopefully take in that at least one person DOES like you, so the thought is not really very true. Or, if you have an extreme thought, like "Then I will wind up homeless and no one will take me in," you can ask yourself how often this has happened to you in the past and how many of your friends and relatives are homeless. Hopefully this will be comforting and will make the thought feel less true.

Give it a try a few times with the blank worksheet in the Appendix and see if it helps. Enjoy playing detective!

16

Gratitude

I think this chapter will compete for being the cheesiest chapter

in this book. Get ready! The goal of this chapter is to share both a

behavioral and a cognitive strategy for changing your mood. This will

work best for sadness and disappointment, but it can also help if you

are feeling angry, frustrated, or resentful.

The topic for today is gratitude. I think I can almost read your

mind right now. You are thinking, "Oh My God. How boring! My parents

always talk about being grateful for stuff and some of my teachers

won't shut up about it, and of course it's good to be grateful. Do I really

have to read about it, too!?"

Gratitude is one of those things everyone pays lip service to and

very few people actually do anything about. But it turns out that you

can use this concept to boost your mood significantly, often with only a

minute or two of effort. Also, there are absolutely no side effects to

feeling grateful, and there is no one out there railing against it.

What do I mean when I talk about "gratitude"? Let's start with

what I DON'T mean. I'm not talking about when you are eating green beans at dinner and you don't want to eat any more, and your father says, "There are starving children in China. You should be grateful you have these green beans!" That would be something like "forced gratitude," and I don't recommend it.

Instead, I am referring to those moments when you, of your own volition, feel happy or excited or fortunate that something is the way it is in your life. This can include very brief things, like feeling grateful that a bite of ice cream tastes delicious or that a perfume smells wonderful. One can be grateful for a smile from someone, getting to class right before the bell rings, or a compliment.

One can also be grateful for material items. At this very moment, I feel grateful that I have a simple, lightweight tent from REI; I have a clean shirt that fits me; I have a snowboard I'm excited about; and I have a roof that has no leaks in it that allows me to stay dry every night. You might feel grateful about owning a certain pair of shoes, a piece of jewelry, or anything else.

There is no limit to the types of things you could theoretically feel grateful for at any given moment. It could be your relationship with a particular friend. You might feel glad that you were not born with Down syndrome. You could feel fortunate that you were born at all. If you are feeling whimsical, you might think about how awesome it is that gravity is a constant and that you don't have to constantly wonder how hard to press off the ground when you walk or if you will float out into space. You might think about how different things would be if there was a large predator animal that hunted humans and how challenging your life would be if you had to constantly hide or evade this predator. Use your imagination.

"Yes, yes, there are lots of things to be grateful for. Whatever. What's your point? I know that already!"

So, most of us would probably agree at this point that there is a nearly endless number of things that one could feel grateful for. But why bother spending time on this, and what does this have to do with depression!? I'll tell you.

Depression is caused by a number of factors, but by far one of the most significant is distorted, negative thoughts. What we focus on and how we interpret events dramatically affects how we feel. The problem is that for nearly any situation, there are many possible things to focus on, and our brains frequently focus on what we don't have or don't like.

Let me give you an example. Pretend you decide to see a movie this weekend. Imagine you see an amazing action movie in IMAX and 3D, the acting is generally great, the special effects are incredible, and you get exactly the seat you want in the theater. Imagine, however, that one of the character's acting felt forced and you wished it were better. How will you think about this movie later?

The person who is depressed may think to themselves later, "Yeah, the movie was pretty good, but that one actor was terrible. They just weren't convincing. They need to step up their acting." And that will be how they summarize the evening in their mind. How do you think they might feel after they have this thought?

In contrast, someone else might see the exact same movie and think, "That movie was awesome! Pretty good acting, one guy could have been a little better, the 3D part was fun, I loved the special effects, and the IMAX made the movie so much better." How do you think this person might feel after recalling this memory?

In any event, we have a choice about what we focus on, and this will dramatically affect how we feel. The world will always have lots of problems—this will not change in our lifetimes. There will always be more war than many of us would prefer, more people acting in a cruel way, wonderful people having awful medical diseases, and children that don't have access to high quality schools or food. Even if ALL of those things were somehow changed, there would still be things one could complain about. Getting older, losing things or people that we care about, knowing we will eventually die. This is an inevitable part of life— that there will be things that we wish were different.

Gratitude is about taking a few seconds to focus on a thing or several things that are going well. This doesn't mean putting your head in the sand and ignoring problems. Nor does it mean being complacent and resting on our laurels for years. I am a huge fan of taking action in the world to make improvements for humanity. But if you spend every waking moment thinking about how messed up things are, you will burn out. I guarantee it. You will feel resentful and helpless and miserable. Don't take my word for it. Talk to people who constantly focus on the negative and how bad things are and see how happy and energized they are.

Spending just a minute or two thinking about some things that are wonderful is rejuvenating. It changes your perspective. Instead of feeling like a victim, you can feel fortunate that some things are going well for you. The downside to doing this is that for a minute or two, you may not feel like a victim. The upside is that you may feel happier and more excited about life.

For any given item, we can always think about people who have it better than we do. But we can also think about people who have it worse than we do. In the world of Behavioral Economics, these are referred to as "Upward Counterfactuals" and "Downward Counterfactuals." An Upward Counterfactual is when you compare yourself to someone or something that is better than you in some way. You might think, "Sure, I live in a house, but Tommy's house is so much bigger than mine. I have it rough." The opposite, a Downward Counterfactual, is when you think about how much worse things could be or how other people don't have it as good as you do. This would be, "Sure, there might be people out there with bigger houses than me, but at least my family HAS a house. There are many homeless people in the world who are at the mercy of the elements and wish that they had a reliable way to stay dry and safe. How wonderful that I don't have to worry about that right now." Both of those perspectives are equally true, but only the Downward Counterfactual will help lift your depression.

At this point, you may or may not buy that different counterfactuals affect your mood differently and profoundly. Let's do a

221

trial so you can see if this is true or not for you. Start with rating your

baseline sadness at this very moment. It might be anywhere from 0 to

100%. Write that down here:

Sadness (Before Upward Counterfactual): _____%

Don't continue until you have written in a number above. Now I

would like you to write down four things that you own or aspects of

yourself that you think other people have it better than you. For

example, you might write "Kaitlin has a nicer car than I do" or "Julio is

smarter than I am." Write those down here right now.

1. _____

_____

2. _____

_____

3. _____

_____

4. _____

   _____

Now that you have done this, think about how sad you are at this

very moment.

Ignore how you felt earlier today, and just think about how you

feel right now. Write this down below.

Sadness (After Upward Counterfactual): _____%

Now, we are going to try something different. Before we start, we want to get another baseline on how you are feeling. If you just finished the exercise on the previous page, your answer will probably be the same as it was a few seconds ago. If it has changed or if you took a break before coming to this paragraph, that's OK too. Write down your sadness at this very moment below.

Sadness (Before Downward Counterfactual): _____%

For the next exercise, we are going to practice a gratitude exercise, which is very similar to a Downward Counterfactual. Think about something that you have that is either better than what someone else has or is something that they don't have at all. Some examples might be "I am better at math than Sam" or "I have a phone, and many people my age don't have a phone at all." Write those down here.

1. _____

   _____

2. _____

_____

3. _____

_____

4. _____

_____

Independent of how your mood was at any other point during today, what is your sadness level at this very moment? Write that down below.

Sadness (After Downward Counterfactual): _____%

Now, compare your sadness level before and after doing the Upward Counterfactual. What did you notice? How about your sadness before and after the Downward Counterfactual? What most people find is that they feel worse when they think about how much better other people have it and better when they think about things that are going well for them. If you found the opposite, or hardly any change, then it might be that gratitude is not currently something that works that well for you. You are welcome to try out some of the suggestions below for a week or so and see if that changes, or you can scrap it and use other techniques instead. Both are fine. If you found that consciously thinking about things you are grateful for was helpful, keep reading.

The challenge is that our brains tend to drift toward the Upward Counterfactual. By default, we naturally think about how our lives could be better than they are and people who have more amazing lives than us. It takes deliberate effort to think about how our situation could be worse or people that have it tougher than we do.

This is where having a habit or ritual that encourages us to do Downward Counterfactuals is valuable. If we aren't mindful, we can spend literally hours in a row ruminating about how bad our lives are. This is rarely helpful but can be hard to get out of, because it feels so true. However, if you have a ritual around gratitude that you do at a particular time during the day, no matter how you are feeling, this can pull you out of a rut.

There are several choices if you decide to try such a ritual. Some people like writing down three things that they are grateful for right before they go to bed at night. The key is to frequently come up with new things, so that it stays fresh rather than stale and forced. Other people like doing this right when they wake up.

In my Dialectical Behavior Therapy Consultation Group, a few weeks ago someone gave us the following Mindfulness exercise. For exactly two minutes, we took a piece of paper and wrote down all the things and people that we are grateful for in our life right now. I was surprised by how many things I came up with, and I noticed feeling happier afterward for several hours. You might try this and see how it goes.

Another option is to pair a ritual with meals. This one doesn't require any writing, and I have enjoyed doing this exercise for the past few years. It's very simple. Before you take a bite of your food, you say out loud one or a few things that you are grateful for. They can be small or large and about anything. It can also be about things you don't have to do, such as "I am grateful I didn't have to go out and hunt this animal myself and that someone did it for me" or "I am grateful that I didn't have to spend hours in a field picking this fruit, and I'm glad that someone did this so that I can enjoy this food." Again, the key is to come up with enough new items that it feels fresh and genuine. If you are alive and have a mouth that is capable of chewing, there are absolutely some things that you could feel grateful for, so you may just need to think creatively if you're struggling to come up with things that are going well for you.

Gratitude can also be a cognitive strategy. If you are trying to defeat a negative thought, sometimes the key is to focus on the things that did go well during an event or the positive qualities in another person or how much worse things could be than they are right now.

The bottom line is that regularly taking time to focus on what you are grateful for can be one of the components of a healthy mood and life. The major problem is not that there are any drawbacks to this practice, but, like working out or meditating, you have to remember to do it and make the effort to incorporate it into your life. I recommend trying one (or several) of the above-mentioned methods for a week or two, and if you find it beneficial, try to make this a routine.

I am grateful that you took the time to read this chapter and that I can now go and eat some lunch!

17

Service and Depression

One of the hallmarks of most animals is that when we feel threatened, we go into "survival mode" and focus on our own safety and security. If there is someone nearby that we are closely related to, such as a child, parent, or sibling, we might muster enough resources to also take their well-being into account. But all other priorities shut down. When we feel overwhelmed or in jeopardy, we become hyperfocused on ourselves and our own well-being.

When we are feeling very sad or depressed, this can take over all aspects of our lives and our thoughts. We can ruminate for hours about how bad our lives are or how horrible our situation is. If I had to put a label on it, I would say that a hallmark of depression is that it tends to make us "self-centered" while we are in its grip.

If being self-centered in this way were an effective way of conserving resources and shortly emerging from the situation, I would be a big fan. But that is not how it tends to go in depression. Think about yourself or someone you know who has been very depressed for at least a few weeks in a row. What tends to happen? In my clinical experience, it usually starts with the depressed person having less bandwidth than usual. They find it harder to do things that used to be fairly straightforward, like calling friends back or texting them. Then they might stop having meals or going out with other people. If they are in a relationship, they often put less effort into interacting with a partner, and the relationship becomes less rewarding. Next to go are often standing commitments, such as church, sports teams, community service, and chores around the house. Eventually, school and work also suffer as the depressed person has even less energy and motivation than before, and things feel pointless and hopeless.

The problem here is that the self-centeredness can start a vicious cycle that is difficult to emerge from. If we put less effort into maintaining relationships with others, we quickly feel isolated and lonely. This leads to more negative thoughts and rumination. We spend hours thinking about ourselves and our situation. This depletes energy further, and we put even less effort into things. Then, we can feel guilty and ashamed that we are not even doing basic things that are expected of us, which contributes to more negative thoughts and a greater sense of inadequacy and inferiority. Quickly, this can lead to not even leaving one's house, laying in bed for many hours during the day, and more feelings of worthlessness and hopelessness. The longer this goes on, often the worse it gets. We can become irritable and short-tempered, pushing away those trying to help, creating even more isolation and loneliness. Then we spend more hours thinking about our terrible situation. The self-centeredness begets more self-centeredness.

The good news is that there are several antidotes for this situation. We have already discussed many, including getting out of bed independent of tiredness, exercising, meditating, gratitude, and writing down your negative thoughts and defeating them with cognitive strategies. I would like to propose another arrow to add to your quiver. A great antidote to self-centeredness is deliberately being other-centered.

The most effective way of being other-centered is deliberately trying to do something with the purpose of serving someone else. I believe that it is nearly impossible to stay depressed while you are giving out sandwiches to homeless people and seeing the gratitude on their faces or taking care of an animal that has been rescued and needs help. If you are hammering in nails to build a home for someone who would otherwise have no home, you will not that minute wonder if your life makes a difference in the world or if you are capable of doing important things. When you put all of your energy into an endeavor that serves others, there is no space left over in the mind for rumination or self-centeredness.

One of the most heartbreaking moments in my recent life was when a charming, funny, likeable 22-year-old told me that he thought his parents would have been better off if he had never been born. He felt worthless, inadequate, and like a complete failure, because he was depressed and was taking longer than he wanted to finish college. Tears are coming to my eyes as I remember his face and how anguished he felt at being inferior and not having any purpose.

One of the interventions that we decided upon was for him to start doing community service. He had been spending many hours per day alone in his room, thinking about how bad his life was and how hopeless things were. We spent part of the session looking up service opportunities in his area, and he decided to prepare food for homeless people through Loaves and Fishes and help build houses through Habitat for Humanity. Within a couple of weeks of these activities, the results were dramatic. He was showering every day, he started going to classes again, his mood was visibly brighter, and his wonderful sense of humor came back. I believe a large part of this improvement was that he went from being fairly self-focused to being more other-focused. In addition to serving those less fortunate than himself, he started getting back in touch with the friends and family he had been ignoring for weeks and began strengthening his social support network. This contributed to him feeling more connected to others, which also improved his mood.

I believe that all of us want to find meaning and purpose in this world. And I don't know anyone I respect whose highest purpose is their own self-improvement. We want to feel that we are contributing to "the greater good" and leaving the world a better place than we found it. When we are only focused on our own needs and thoughts and desires for a long time, happiness is usually elusive. Even the greatest sources of hedonic pleasure are rarely sufficient for long-term happiness.

I believe one of the best ways that you can make yourself feel better is to go out and do something to help someone or something else. It doesn't have to be "altruistic." I hate that word. I don't care what your motivations are. Mine are often selfish. I know that helping others makes me feel good, so I do it. This is not because I am more evolved or sacrificing than others. I know that my history has shown that when I buy someone else a cup of coffee or a sandwich or provide support for someone in need, I feel better than I did before. That's my primary motivation. I'm nervous that people might judge me for that, but it's the honest truth. A "side effect" of my actions is that other people might feel happier, but my main driving force is that I like feeling generous and believing that my life has purpose.

Don't take my word for it. I believe in experimentation, and I think everyone should test things out for themselves. Run an experiment. First, you always want to get a baseline. There are many emotions we could choose from for this test, but how about "worthlessness"? Write down exactly how worthless you feel on a scale of 0 to 100% below.

Worthless: _____%

Now, let's pick something you can do right now that would make the world a better place. The choices are nearly limitless. Let's start small. If you are within ten minutes of a coffee shop, take this book with you and go to said coffee shop. Get in line, turn to the person in front of or behind you, and say, "Excuse me, are you getting a beverage?" If they say yes, say, "Could I get that for you, please?" They will probably be surprised, perhaps even a little suspicious that you have ulterior motives. That's OK. If they express hesitation, you can add something like, "This is just something I like to do sometimes. You would be making my day better if I could buy you a beverage. No strings attached." This is usually sufficient, and the person may be smiling by now. If they say no, go to the next person in line and repeat the same spiel. Eventually, someone will say yes. When they do, order exactly what they want or let them order it, then pay for it. Then say something like, "Have a good day." That's it.

If you are not near a coffee shop or you are feeling inspired to do something different, that is great, too. Some of my clients like to occasionally write a short letter to someone they are grateful to expressing how much they have benefited from knowing that person. Marty Seligman, father of the "Positive Psychology" movement, then recommends that you deliver the letter to the recipient in person and have them read it while you are right there. There are small studies showing that this act alone can produce increased happiness for several weeks. If that feels like too much right now, sending the letter by email or snail mail is also wonderful, and even if you never send it, just the act of writing it can feel good.

If you are reading this and are near other people, you could also pick anyone (including strangers), walk up to them, and give them a genuine compliment. Find something about them that you like or admire, such as their hair or an item of clothing or jewelry, and tell them how much you like that thing. Most of us don't get nearly enough compliments in our ordinary life, so this will probably feel surprising and warm to the person receiving your gift, and they may smile.

If you are an animal lover, there are lots of great options. If you have a four-legged creature around, you can go pet them and give them some love and attention and see how they respond. Most domestic animals love being touched, and in addition to you feeling good about yourself for making their day better, you will also get a burst of oxytocin (a chemical that is released in your brain when you are experiencing touch that feels good).

If you live with your parents or a roommate, doing a chore out of the blue is a wonderful act of service. Without being asked, do something that you don't have to do but you know might make the house nicer or make someone else's life easier. Take out the trash. Or wash a couple of dishes. Or vacuum one room. Or cut up a fruit or vegetable and ask if anyone would like some. These don't have to be fancy. Even a very small act can be exciting to others in your area, particularly when it's unexpected and voluntary.

If you are feeling really ambitious and inspired, one of my favorite activities when I'm feeling down is to find a homeless person nearby, ask them if they are hungry, and walk with them to a nearby store and buy them some food. If you do this, in the middle you may have a string of thoughts like "Should I really be doing this? Am I enabling an unhealthy lifestyle? Am I delaying them getting better? What did they do to become homeless? Do they really deserve this food? Blah blah blah!" Ignore those thoughts. They are not very useful right now. I recommend in that situation saying something to yourself along these lines: "The odds are good that at this moment, the person next to me is suffering more than I am. The five or ten dollars I am spending right now will probably not make a huge difference in my life today, but this person may experience a great amount of happiness if I buy them food out of the blue. I will trust that this is a 'good' act and just do it, even if I have some reservations." Then, buy them a sandwich or a meal. Even if they are not at all grateful, you will know that you just made their day better and you are helping the human race. And it is completely fine that your primary motivation is for YOU to feel better—

it is still a wonderful act and will likely improve your own mood. (Note

to reader: my editor wisely advises here that I should mention it's best

to do acts of service in a public place with other people around, and

trust your instincts if anything feels off. But if you follow those

guidelines, you should be fine.)

So, spend a minute or two thinking about what act you want to

do RIGHT NOW. If you are pressed for time, I recommend buying

someone coffee or giving a compliment. It doesn't really matter what

you choose. I just want you to pick something, and go do it. Even if you

are feeling nervous, even if you have social anxiety, even if you are

worried you will get "rejected," even if you are tired, do it anyway. Trust

me. This is the only way to know if this act will help you or not. Please

do not go on reading until you have done something that benefited

someone or something else. Seriously. This is not a spectator sport. Just

go do it! Then, immediately after, write down your current level of

feeling worthless.

To be completed AFTER an act of service: Worthless: _____%

Do not go on to the next page until you have completed the above.

Hello. Did you do the act of service just now? I didn't think so. I'm onto you! You thought you could just read these pages passively and still feel a whole lot better. It doesn't work that way! It's like reading a book about weight loss but not doing any exercises. You have to take an active role in your own recovery if you want to get better. No one can do it for you. If you didn't do an act of service and just flipped to the next page, please go back to the last page and don't come back until you've done it and written in your percentage.

Thank you! How did that feel? What was your "worthlessness" score before compared to after? Most of my clients have found that it's quite hard to feel worthless while or right after you are serving others. This makes sense, right? Of course you are not worthless. Not only do you have intrinsic worth by being a human being, but you just did something that made someone or something's life better than it was. What could be more worthwhile than that?

The bad news is that the effects of any intervention, including doing nice things for others, wear off eventually. The good news is that you can do it again! I assure you that there is no shortage of opportunities to make the world a better place.

If you are at least partially buying this idea that doing things for others makes us feel good, please experiment and see which forms of service work best for you. You may need to do some trial and error. If you are currently out of work or not in school, this could be a great opportunity since you have more free time on your hands. Try spending an hour or two at a soup kitchen serving food to homeless people. If you are in high school, you could join a club that does community service activities. If you are in college, you could find a local program in which you tutor or mentor younger kids. The Big Brothers/Big Sisters program is always looking for volunteers. The Ronald McDonald house allows you to support families who have a child getting treatment for cancer. Habitat for Humanity allows you to get some fresh air and learn how to build a house for someone in need, even if you don't know what you're doing at all. I have fond memories of spending every Saturday for a year in Washington D.C. building a house, and they were very patient with my lack of knowledge and skills! If you are over 21, you might consider joining a service club in your community, like Rotary, as these allow you to do service and also make new friends.

At this point, you might be on board with believing that doing service for others helps our own mood, but you might be wondering why this is the case. I have a few explanations. The first is that depression leads to rumination and hours of thinking negative thoughts. Just about anything that breaks that cycle and gets you doing something else is valuable. Serving others is at the very least a distraction from thinking about our own troubles.

But service is also more than just a distraction. It is a reminder that there are those who are less fortunate than us. This doesn't mean that we are better or superior. It means we are truly fortunate that events went well enough in our lives that we have the capacity to do something that benefits others. When you come into contact with a person or animal that is suffering, and you spend time with them, you can appreciate how much worse things could be for you right now. I can't even tell you the number of days that I have driven to work thinking about my own problems in my life, and they felt huge and tremendously important. Then, within about a minute of listening to someone in my office who was physically abused, or raped, or tried to kill themselves, suddenly my problems didn't seem so large anymore. It is humbling and important to realize that there are those who have larger or different problems than we do. Providing compassion or support to those who are suffering helps us put our own lives into perspective, which can combat depression.

Also, when we see a smile on someone's face and believe that we helped make their day a little better or a little easier, we gain a sense of competence and skillfulness. It is terrible believing that we are incompetent or inadequate. When we see that we have changed the world, even a tiny bit, we can feel a small sense of accomplishment. And then we can accomplish other things. Believing that we have agency in the world and the ability to impact our environment is another necessary condition for overcoming depression, and doing service can help provide that.

Finally, one of my favorite aspects of helping others is that it helps us feel more connected to other people and the world. This section will probably come off as new-agey and cheesy, but I'm going to write it anyway. We are all connected to each other. We have all experienced suffering, we all bleed, we all get sick, and we all wish to be happy. It is very sad to me that our brains spend so much energy and attention on our differences, and we get deluded into thinking that we are more different from each other than we are similar.

This is the biggest delusion our mind can perpetrate. My favorite Einstein quote is the following:

"A human being is a part of the whole called by us universe, a part limited in time and space. He experiences himself, his thoughts and feeling as something separated from the rest, a kind of optical delusion of his consciousness. This delusion is a kind of prison for us, restricting us to our personal desires and to affection for a few persons nearest to us. Our task must be to free ourselves from this prison by widening our circle of compassion to embrace all living creatures and the whole of nature in its beauty."

When we deliberately help others, we are reminded that we are not as different as we typically assume. We are interdependent on each other. Not a person alive today would be where they are unless one or more people fed them when they were a baby, clothed them, and took care of them. When we help others, we set off ripples in the universe. We can positively affect how that person interacts with other people, even just a little, and sometimes these ripples can affect numerous people. When we get caught up in our own thoughts, we can feel lonely and disconnected. Loving and serving other people allows us to feel part of something greater. It gives us meaning and purpose.

As a final clarification, I don't want to give the impression that I am against "self-care" or selfishness in certain contexts. Selfishness can

244

actually be incredibly healthy. Taking 10 or 20 minutes to meditate in the morning can be rejuvenating and peaceful. Getting a massage can be very relaxing after a difficult time. Taking time to do a hobby you enjoy might be purely for your own enjoyment, and that is great. In fact, if you only spend every single minute focused on doing your job or helping others, you may well burn out.

I am advocating balance. There is a paradox here. If you spend some time each day doing things that are relaxing or pleasurable for you, you are more likely to feel happy and calm. I recommend this. If you are feeling calm and energized, you are more likely to have energy left over for others. And then when you do something that benefits nature or animals or humans, I believe you are more likely to feel satisfied and even more energized. This, too, can become a cycle. Some of my favorite stories are of people who get excited and passionate about a project or activity that benefits the world, which feeds back into their own energy and creativity.

The challenge here is that your brain will trick you into thinking that you don't have enough energy or money or time to do anything that benefits others. This is a lie! A distortion. It is simply not true. It is like looking at a star in the night sky. You think you are looking at an object that is a few miles away, when you are actually looking at light that traveled many years to hit your eye at that moment—light from an object that may not even actually exist anymore. But it feels very true that you are seeing the star as it is right now. It is a trick.

The same is true when you think that you can't summon the energy to do service. Particularly if you are depressed (but also when we are stressed or angry or overwhelmed), you will think that you couldn't possibly do something for someone else when you are already so taxed.

The secret is to test this hypothesis. Go out and see what happens if you find another human being and give them a compliment. See what happens if you buy a stranger lunch out of the blue. You will not think that you can do this, but it is well worth trying.

What I recommend is to start small. If you got this far in the chapter, you probably already did at least one small act of service. Go do that again tomorrow. Or something different. It is quite reasonable to get a few small acts under your belt and feel a sense of accomplishment rather than to start with signing up for the Peace Corps. Check in with yourself before and after you do something for others and see how you feel. I think you will find that this was more doable than you believed and that you now feel somewhat better.

In the event that even doing a small act proved impossible, you probably would benefit from professional treatment with a qualified therapist. One great resource is the Feeling Good Institute (www.feelinggoodinstitute.com). The therapists on this website excel at TEAM therapy, which can be very effective for depression. If you are struggling with doing some of the basic exercises in this book, you might need additional support.

If you start integrating some acts of service into your life, I predict you will find that this can be a powerful antidote to depression. You will be distracting yourself from your negative thoughts, realizing that your situation could be worse than it is, gaining a sense of agency in the world, and hopefully feeling more connected to the universe. If other people, animals, or nature get the added bonus of benefiting from your deeds, that's not too shabby either. Thank you for any positive acts you have already done or will do soon. My heart is warmed knowing that you are helping to make the world better than it would have been without your service.

18

Relapse Prevention

Hopefully, by the time you are reading this, you are feeling significantly better than when you started this book. In an ideal world, you are now exercising regularly, meditating in the mornings, getting a healthy amount of sleep, and maybe even practicing some gratitude or service to others. You have a few cognitive techniques that you know how to apply when your thoughts are distorted. You are starting to get a little better at staying in the moment and not paying as much attention to distracting negative thoughts. It is even possible that your depression has completely lifted and you are having more days than not in which you generally feel happy.

If you are frequently feeling happy and not weighed down by anxious or upsetting thoughts, you are (as my mentor David Burns is fond of saying) "in a state of enlightenment." This phrase is only half-joking. There are many definitions and constructs of "enlightenment." When I use the term, I am referring to a state in which a person is aware of what is happening in their life, generally happy, and not engaging in distorted thinking. These moments can be quite wonderful. When I am "in a state of enlightenment," I usually feel relaxed and excited about the future, and small setbacks don't affect me too much. You may have experienced some minutes like this in the past, and it's possible you are even in a state of enlightenment at this very moment!

It's also possible that you are currently feeling pretty crappy. If that is the case, you may want to do some quick "troubleshooting." Go back and skim over the earlier chapters, and see if you are doing everything recommended COMPLETELY. That means a daily meditation practice, five to six days a week of 30 to 90 minutes of exercise, at least eight hours of sleep, and ideally some gratitude, doing kind things for others, and some social time. If you decided to skip any of those or do them halfheartedly, that might be your problem. Figure out which of those you are not doing, reread that chapter, and make it a regular habit. If you're struggling doing it on your own, perhaps contact a trained professional in TEAM therapy, and they can help you with these habits.

If you are doing ALL of the aforementioned practices, it might be that you are having some distorted thoughts. If that is the case, write down the thoughts you are having at this moment. Do NOT try to do this in your head. You will be tempted to do this in your head, and then it won't work. Trust me. Write down the thoughts, then use some of the cognitive techniques we have gone over and see if your feelings change. If not, you may need to learn a few more cognitive techniques. Feel free to buy *Feeling Good: The New Mood Therapy* to get a few more tricks under your belt. If you have tried at least 20 techniques and none of them are working, you may want to get professional help from someone who can teach you these skills in depth.

If you are reading this and you are generally feeling pretty good right now, congratulations! This is wonderful. Life is short, and if you are having some minutes of feeling happy and reasonably relaxed, savor it! Life is also quite hard, in my opinion, and having even a short time of relief from our buzz of negative thoughts is a delightful experience. Enjoy your time in enlightenment.

Now, not to kill your buzz, but I have some bad news. You're probably not going to like what I have to say right now, but I have to be upfront with you and prepare you for the inevitable. You ready? Here is the bad news: No one is entitled to permanently stay in a state of enlightenment.

This idea might be upsetting to you. You might have hoped that if you diligently followed every recommendation in this book and learned every technique, you would be riding high on a cloud of euphoria that would last the rest of your life. No such luck. If I could offer that to you, I would! That sounds lovely. But this is not the fate of human beings. We suffer, and we fall "out" of enlightenment. If you experience even a minute of sadness or worry, let's call that a "relapse." I am deliberately being vague about the length of time and severity of the relapse that you might experience, but let's say that just about any amount of time that you are feeling upset counts as a relapse.

When this happens to you, and you go back to buying into your negative thoughts and feeling down, it doesn't mean you have necessarily done anything wrong. Even if you are rigorous in your daily regimen of healthy habits, at some time or another you will get sucked into distorted thinking. It happens to all of us, and it's rough. Sometimes we stop doing healthy habits like exercising, meditating, or sleeping well, and we are then more vulnerable to negative thoughts and life events. Other times we experience a very real and profound loss in our lives, such as the death of a loved one, and we appropriately feel quite sad. Most commonly, we pay attention to the thoughts that emerge from our brain, and when we buy into the distorted ones that tell us that things should be different than they are, we suffer. That is the bad news.

But, you have probably picked up on my optimism from previous chapters and maybe intuited that I wouldn't leave you with this morbid pronouncement as my final word on the subject of enlightenment. There are also several pieces of GOOD news!

The first bit of good news is that we can always come back to a state of enlightenment. No matter what events have occurred in your life, no matter what choices you have made previously, you have the power to feel differently at this very moment. You can do a "reset." No matter how bad things are right now, you have a choice to put these strategies into action and feel dramatically different than you have been feeling. I find that concept both comforting and liberating.

The second piece of good news is that the severity of any future relapses you experience need not be as severe as your depression has been in the past. Although I cannot protect you from having at least several minutes of sadness, worry, jealousy, anger, and all the other negative emotions, they need not affect you as severely as before. You can use behavioral and cognitive strategies to reduce the force of these thoughts and emotions.

The final morsel of good news is perhaps the most important.

The "relapses" that you will experience in the future do not need to last very long. In fact, they could conceivably be under an hour for the rest of your life! I recognize this is a bold claim, but it's true. If you recognize early that you are feeling sad or upset or resentful, you can immediately take steps to change how you are feeling and nip the relapse in the bud!

There is one exception to this that I want to highlight for a moment. The exception is when you experience a significant loss. When this happens, you will not feel sad for less than an hour. In fact, you might feel quite sad for days, or even weeks. This can be healthy and often even necessary. Loss can come in many forms in addition to the death of a loved family member, such as the death of a pet, a friend moving away, or the loss of a physical capability, a role, a relationship, or part of our identity.

If you experience a significant loss, I highly recommend that you allow yourself some time to grieve or mourn this loss. This is considered "healthy grief." Allowing yourself time to cry, time to reflect on how much you cared about what was lost, and letting yourself feel whatever emotions show up without "pushing them away" is essential. This can be quite challenging but will ultimately allow you to move on with your life if you allow this process to occur.

However, in normal, ordinary conditions, a relapse need only last for minutes at a time. If you recall from the chapter on "Cognitive Therapy," it is not the events in our lives that determine our happiness, but our thoughts and interpretations of these events. In nearly any situation, short of being physically tortured, it is possible to gain some perspective on our situation and accept what is happening without being very bothered by it.

Let me give you an example to illustrate these concepts. I recently finished 20 hours of pro bono therapy with a wonderful young man named Jamal. Jamal is a 17-year-old African American boy who is currently in the foster system after experiencing physical and sexual abuse at the hands of his parents, maternal grandparents, and paternal grandparents. Jamal was removed from his parents' custody at the age of four, when they were both heavily into methamphetamine and unable to care for him properly. He had recently been experiencing significant depression, anxiety, relationship problems, and low motivation to do anything. He called me out of the blue a couple of months ago saying that he found me on the Internet, he needed help, and he didn't have any money, but he wondered if there was any chance I could help him.

Jamal shared with me that he had dreams of going to college and becoming a therapist so that he could help those who had been through similar circumstances. His story tugged at my heartstrings, and I decided to see him for a 20-hour Intensive for free. I felt a little nervous that since he had been through so much, perhaps my usual strategies and techniques would not be sufficient to help him, but we decided it was worth a try.

I told Jamal on the phone that if I agreed to see him, he was going to have to work his butt off if we were going to get anywhere. He would have to read the books I would ask him to read, exercise regularly, start meditating, show up on time for all our long sessions, and work hard in therapy to get the most out of it. He accepted wholeheartedly and seemed grateful for my willingness to work with him.

Jamal took the bus over an hour every day to see me and showed up early for all our sessions. He was courageously vulnerable with me and recounted awful tales of abuse that he had experienced. We had times when all he did was cry and sit with the sadness of what he had gone through, and tears came to my eyes as well. Part of our work was grieving the loss of the parenting that he had wanted in his life and not received, and he sat with these feelings of sadness and anger without pushing them away.

We also went over numerous behavioral strategies for how to change emotions and about a dozen cognitive techniques for how to change his thoughts. We role-played more effective ways of communicating with others. Jamal had also kept his guard up with friends, not telling them about his past, because he had been hurt so many times by others that it made sense to avoid vulnerability. Paradoxically, this constant guardedness kept people at a distance and made him feel lonelier, and we talked about how to practice being more vulnerable and authentic with others and learning to take chances trusting other people. We covered procrastination and motivation, and he started meditating daily and being more efficient with his time.

By the end of the Intensive, Jamal's depression and anxiety were down to zero. He had periods of feeling quite happy, even laughing, and this was very rewarding to witness. All seemed to be going even better than both of us could have imagined.

But then he had a relapse. Shortly before the end of our treatment together, Jamal became quite sad. He expressed to me that he was worried about losing me and going on in the world without seeing me regularly. He said, "No one has ever been this nice to me, and I haven't opened up with anyone this much before." His feelings were real, and he felt scared that this sadness would last forever.

However, instead of dwelling in the sadness indefinitely, he was able to recognize that there were things in his power he could do to change his feelings. He started by accepting that he was feeling sad, that this was quite natural, and he allowed himself to experience this without pushing it away. Paradoxically, this ended up eventually making the sadness less intense. Then he thought about some things that he was grateful for, including the friendship of his sister, having a place to live, and our work together. Finally, he wrote down some of these thoughts and was able to change them and feel more hopeful about the future.

The next day we discussed what relapse is and how he dealt with it. We were able to see that already he was gaining the power to change his feelings without me, and he found this empowering. After we ended his treatment, I received one of the best letters that I have ever read. Jamal wrote to me about how much happier he was feeling, enrolling in community college, and feeling less angry and resentful. I still look at this letter sometimes and feel grateful that Jamal not only felt better by the end of our sessions, but also that he learned the skills of relapse prevention and how to get out of negative moods on his own.

For this final section of the chapter, I would like to give you a quick "algorithm" of what to do if you find yourself in a relapse. First, remind yourself that at any time you can get back into a state of enlightenment, and just by noticing that you are feeling off, you are beginning the steps of changing how you feel. Secondly, ask yourself if you have just experienced a significant loss. If so, allow yourself to feel sad for some time, as this is healthy and appropriate. If this is not the source of your upset, do an assessment of your last week or two and see if you have been diligently doing healthy habits or if you have fallen out of exercising, meditating, sleeping at least eight hours, or doing some form of gratitude practice and/or service to others. If any of those are missing, go back to doing them all daily and make this your primary focus.

If you have been engaging in consistent healthy habits and are still feeling upset, try allowing yourself to experience whatever emotion you are feeling without pushing it away. Do this for at least 10-20 minutes and see what happens. If nothing changes, I recommend trying the strategy of "Throwing Yourself Fully into an Activity." This is the same as being Mindful, meaning that you put all your energy into going for a run, or washing dishes, or talking to a friend, or listening to a teacher, or anything else. When you completely stay present in any activity, it is much harder to have room for negative thoughts, and this alone is a powerful antidote to depression and anxiety. Do this for at least one hour, and then check in and see how you feel.

If you are still feeling anxious or upset, try writing down all the thoughts that are upsetting you and how strong your different emotions are. Then figure out all the advantages of holding on to a given thought, then all the disadvantages. If you still want to change that thought, try a number of cognitive strategies to defeat the thought. If you stick with it and keep trying many different strategies, you will likely feel better.

To summarize, all of us go "in and out of enlightenment" many times throughout our life. The important thing is to recognize that you have the power to change your own thoughts and feelings and that if you practice healthy habits and write down your negative thoughts, you can go back to feeling happy and relaxed at any time. And when you experience those moments of enlightenment, savor them!

19

From Despair to Normalcy to Contentment, Meaning,

Excitement, and Connection

You may have noticed that the focus of this book has been on getting over depression. The great majority of the chapters have been designed to get a teenager or young adult with clinical depression, including those having suicidal thoughts, out of the range of danger and into mental health. If this book helps even one young person who was planning on killing themselves not die by suicide, I believe that will be a tremendous success.

The mental health field has for 99% of its history been defined as "the absence of disease." Doctors love curing diseases, and we usually feel pretty proud of ourselves when we get rid of a pneumonia or a cancer or any other disease. The problem when it comes to applying this concept to brain "diseases" is that it's more complicated. In the case of depression, the absence of disease would mean that you have normal ups and downs and lead a pretty good life, at least one not crippled by lying in bed all the time and feeling terrible. A life feeling "mostly decent" would certainly be better than a life with frequent episodes of depression, but this might also not be your only goal. You may justifiably be aiming higher than that.

This final chapter is about how to go beyond "getting over depression" into normal ups and downs, and pushing through that ceiling. I want to spend at least one chapter showing you how to have a better than average life. I want to guide you in how to achieve contentment, meaning, excitement, and connection in your life.

You might be thinking to yourself at this point, "Dammit! Only one chapter! You spent the entire book just trying to get me to normal ups and downs and then devote one lousy chapter to living the good life. You punk! I want my money back. Well, my parents' money back. Why didn't you spend the whole book on this topic!!!?"

Valid question. You know I'm a sucker for a good analogy, so I'll try one here. Let's pretend there is an island with no physical therapists or doctors and many people with broken legs who are in a lot of pain. If you were one of those people who couldn't walk and were in intense pain all the time, I would be honored to teach you how to make the pain go away and be able to walk normally again. That would be a major accomplishment in my book (get it? ☺). I might stop there. But now pretend that I love to run marathons. Maybe I would also spend a little

261

time showing you how to go beyond normal use of your legs and how to run very fast for long distances. That would be fantastic, too, but we would have to start with getting your leg working normally before getting into the advanced stuff. Yes?

This final chapter is written for those of you who have diligently followed all the previous chapters and gotten to a place where there are no longer weeks in a row of feeling miserable. In an ideal world, if you have been exercising, sleeping well, meditating, doing gratitude exercises and downward counterfactuals, serving others, and doing some cognitive techniques on your written negative thoughts, you are hopefully feeling significantly better. This chapter is about how to go from good to amazing.

Before we begin, I have one caveat. The caveat is that no matter how closely you follow my instructions, you will still have minutes of feeling sad, minutes of feeling worried, minutes of feeling every emotion known to humankind. This is inescapable. I wrote about this extensively in the chapter on "Relapse Prevention," and it still holds true even if you're practicing the "advanced stuff." You are welcome to wish for endless minutes of joy and excitement, but I suspect that if you demand that life provide you with these emotions constantly, you will feel disappointed. I recommend that, as hard as it is to accept this fact, start accepting that emotions are fleeting, everything in life is temporary, and it is a given that no matter how disciplined or thoughtful you are, you will experience minutes of suffering. If you like the broken leg/running analogy, then think of it this way: Even if I taught you how to be a world-class, award-winning marathon runner, at some point in your running career you would still get injured. At some point, you would have a run that didn't go the way you wanted it to, no matter how hard you trained or how fast you were. The paradox of this suffering is that it could help you appreciate those races that did go well—those times you were running at a peak level. If you are willing to accept that, I will try to show you how to have as many minutes as possible experiencing contentment, meaning, excitement, and connection.

Let's start with the concept of "contentment." By contentment, I mean the idea of feeling calm and not at that moment needing anything to be different than it is. In Eastern religions, when the word "happiness" is discussed, it is often the quality of contentment that is being described and encouraged.

Have you ever experienced a few seconds of contentment? Try

to think of a time when you felt calm, relaxed, peaceful, and accepting of what was happening in that moment. Perhaps it was sitting by yourself with a hot beverage, enjoying a few minutes to yourself, sipping liquid warmth, and savoring a brief time before starting something more rigorous. Maybe you raced to get somewhere, felt nervous that you would be late or miss an event, and then experienced a few seconds of relief and peace as you sat down and knew that you could now relax and enjoy the experience. I often experience the most contentment when I am doing sitting meditation in the morning and, for a few minutes, my only task is to focus on my breath and I don't need to worry about anything else or take care of anyone. Those moments are delightful.

There are several reliable methods of achieving more contentment in your life. A daily meditation practice and adequate sleep help tremendously. Not only might you experience contentment during your meditation, but having a more calm and rested mind will also increase the chances of feeling relaxed and at ease during your day.

Another important practice for finding more contentment is doing LESS. I give props to Leo Babauta, author of *The Power of Less,* for helping me finally get why scheduling every minute of every day and saying yes to every invitation was stressing me out for so long. If you are in a hurry and constantly rushing from thing to thing, it is incredibly difficult, if not impossible, to feel "content."

When I was in medical school, I had the opportunity to live in Costa Rica for two months with a host family. I knew no Spanish at the time, and they spoke no English. This rotation allowed me to learn Spanish and also do really selfless things, like lie on the beach for hours and learn to surf.

One of the members of my host family was Alejandro. Alejandro led a simple existence. He woke up, ate some fresh pineapple or mango and some rice and beans. Then he walked five miles to the beach and surfed for a while. Then he taught a surf lesson or two to earn some money. At night, he hung out with his friends and played the guitar. He was one of the happiest guys I ever met.

Part of why Alejandro was so happy was that he had some free time during the day. His life wasn't constantly hurried. He had a good deal of contentment.

Particularly if you are an American reading this, the idea of having "free time" with nothing scheduled might sound ludicrous. You might think I am an idiot for even suggesting something so laughable. If you are a high school student, especially a junior, you might distantly remember "free time" as something you had when you were four.

I'm not going to try to convince you to have more free time in your life. If you have somehow rearranged your life to fit in daily meditation, exercise, and eight hours of sleep, this is already a tremendous accomplishment! You are now probably in the top 3% of people for having healthy habits. I won't pretend to know the details of your specific life or how important your extracurricular activities, grades, or hobbies are to you.

I personally think that life is too challenging for the average high school student. I think that having six or seven hours a day of classes, plus lots of homework, plus an expectation of demonstrated commitment to sports/music/hobbies to get into college is too much!! I wish I could design the world and have more power in this domain. I can assure you that if you are in high school and reading this, it does get better. I promise you! You have some say right now in how many hobbies and sports you do, but even if you cut back on one or more things, it will probably still be hard to find free time. It might just be a little easier with one or two fewer commitments on your plate.

If you are in college or graduate school or working, you probably have a little bit more flexibility with your time. You probably have at least some say in how many classes you take, how many of them have labs, and how many clubs and activities you sign up for. If you are working full-time, you may not realize it, but you do have some say in whether you do the job you have currently or a different job. You also have a decent amount of control over what you do with your free time.

My message to you is that if you would like to experience more contentment, play around with doing less. Scheduling less. Leaving one or more night a week "free" with nothing scheduled. See how you feel on a Saturday when you haven't scheduled anything compared to a Saturday when you have planned five different events. This is a lesson I have to keep learning over and over in life as I tend to schedule too much, and only when I have had several months of feeling harried and rushed and overcommitted do I again renew a commitment to allow more buffer time between things and free time to just read, watch TV, or take care of emergencies. Often less is more.

My final recommendation for a more content life is to recognize a fundamental aspect of the human experience: If we are fully present in the activity we are doing at this moment, we will probably be about as happy as if we were doing some other activity instead. This will also be about as happy as we would be if we were by ourselves or with someone different than we are currently with.

This is a radical idea, and it is also true. It has powerful implications. If this were true, what would this mean in your own life? How often, while you are doing something, do you imagine that things would be so much better if only you were doing something else instead? Write down at least one time recently when you were doing something and imagined how wonderful it would be to be somewhere else or with someone else instead:

1. _____

   _____

2. _____

   _____

Did you write down at least one thing? I bet you didn't. I knew it! You thought we were done with all this demanding writing stuff. Not yet! Go back and write down at least one example above. You're almost done!

What did you come up with? There are numerous possibilities. And I imagine that it felt very true at the time that it would be so much better if you were only doing something different.

The truth is that most things in life have the capacity to be enjoyable and/or satisfying if we are totally present while we are doing them. I have found anecdotally that when my mind is wandering, distorted thoughts often drift in, and I frequently feel worried and/or upset. However, when I "Throw Myself Fully" into writing, or washing dishes, or a conversation, or doing therapy, or almost anything else, I feel about 96% happy. I might still have the distorted thought "But I would be SOOOOO much happier if only I was doing blank or with blank or owned blank. Then things would be awesome!" But, I remind myself that this is a trick my mind is playing on me and is not really true.

You have probably heard the expression "The grass is always greener on the other side of the fence." This is a tongue-in-cheek idea that wherever we are standing, we imagine it is so much more amazing somewhere nearby or doing something a little different. Not true! Certainly, when I am driving (one of my least favorite activities) and paying full attention to driving, I am probably only about 93 or 94% happy. In contrast, when I am having a conversation with one of my

269

best friends, I might be as high as 98% happy. Definitely happier!

I am not contending that every activity is exactly equal in enjoyment. What I am asserting is that they are pretty close when we are engaging mindfully. And doing things by ourselves is often just as enjoyable when we get rid of any distorted thoughts that are contributing to feelings of loneliness. Don't take my word for this, try this at home!

When you are telling yourself that life would be so much better if you were doing something different, try reminding yourself that your capacity for happiness right now is about the same as if you were doing this other thing that sounds so much cooler. This alone may allow you to feel more content in your current situation. Try to relax into it and accept that this is what you are doing right at this moment. Often, once we get rid of the craving and clinging to be doing or having something else, the suffering disappears.

Let's briefly touch on the idea of having more "meaning" in your life. There have been numerous books written on the subject, and they have a lot in common. For example, they all agree (correctly) that if you feel that your life has meaning or purpose, you are more likely to feel fulfilled. And fulfillment is one aspect of happiness.

270

The best news here is that there are many roads that lead to Rome. There are an almost endless number of ways of finding meaning in your life. The most important thing is that you consciously, deliberately set aside some amount of time each day or week or month to do something that you believe will benefit something or someone besides yourself.

This gives you hundreds, if not thousands, of options. You could volunteer to work with animals in a shelter. You could teach children to read. You could get paid to do a job that improves the environment. You could give money to charities that support a cause you believe in. Some people find meaning through religion or spirituality. I personally derive the most joy and meaning when I can directly see that another human has benefited from my action. Whether I am volunteering or getting paid, I take tremendous joy in believing that I just helped someone suffer less or experience more joy in their life.

My final recommendation with regards to having "meaning" is to not get caught up in "quantifying" your impact on the world. I probably wasted several hundred hours wondering if I was doing "enough" to help people in my community, and although it did motivate me to do more service, it also caused me tremendous anxiety and guilt and shame. I was equating my worth with exactly "how much" I was helping others. I feel grateful to David Burns for doing some personal work with me to help me still find tremendous value in serving others, but without basing my "worth" on some "number" of service points I was doing. I also think Timothy Ferriss has an eloquent discussion on this topic in *The 4-Hour Work Week*. He points out that it doesn't really matter whether you are saving the dolphins or saving the children, debating if your cause is better than someone else's cause or has "more impact" is impossible to quantify and is generally a complete waste of time and energy. If you are deliberately doing one or more things that contribute to the greater good, you are helping the world and that is enough.

Excitement is one of my favorite topics, and I may write a whole book on this topic in the future. In my opinion, this is the "bad boy" twin of contentment, and both are part of the greater whole of happiness. I can imagine an alternate universe in which I spend every hour living in a monastery, eating two vegan meals a day, meditating for 12 hours a day, and feeling quite content. I just think I would also be bored! I personally love adrenaline rushes, and having excitement in life is one of my main sources of joy.

The bad news is that pure excitement every minute of every day is unlikely to be sustainable. Eventually, that road will lead you to continually "upping the ante" until you are bungee jumping off a 200-foot crane while having a threesome and shooting up heroin. It sounds very exciting, but I can't imagine you could keep this up for long. You will probably wind up broke, in jail, or dead if you exclusively focus on excitement.

Now that I have scared you silly, I would like to backtrack a bit and argue that a dose of excitement can be "part of a balanced breakfast." If you are mindfully engaging in some simple activities and doing some things that give you meaning in life, it is also healthy to have things to look forward to that you are passionate and excited about.

This too offers numerous options. You might find that for you, going to concerts or music festivals is tremendously exciting. Other people go for shorter thrills, like roller coasters, bungee jumping, or skydiving. Traveling to new places, whether domestic or international, can be novel and enriching. One of my adrenaline-junkie clients enjoys big-wave surfing and kiteboarding. My dad has done an annual backpacking trip in the Sierra Nevada Mountains for the past 30 years, and he loves the time planning for the trip in addition to the camping itself. I get excited about every scuba diving trip I plan. Flirting and dating can provide big dopamine rushes.

It is also quite reasonable to focus on things that are not inherently "exciting" in and of themselves but that you FEEL excited about researching or doing. I dated someone who loved cooking and got excited about finding new recipes. Some people get pumped about learning a new musical instrument. This sounds really nerdy, but even learning about a subject you find intriguing can actually be exciting.

The bottom line is that having things to look forward to and getting excited about upcoming adventures can be part of a satisfying and complete life. If you are not only excited about something in the future, but that event is also exciting, this combination can be even more thrilling. This is best done in moderation, but if you do not currently have hobbies or activities you are passionate about, I recommend trying some of the above items and building some excitement into your regular life.

Finally, I want to put in a plug for "connection" as part of an optimally happy life. Spending time with others, particularly those we care about, can be a powerful antidote to depression. But it can also do more than that. Developing deep, intimate relationships with other people can not only remove a lot of sadness, it can also help you to feel extremely happy and cared for. Let's look at a couple of basic lines of evidence to support this claim.

Humans are primates, and primates are social animals. Our brains are wired to connect with others. No doubt about it. We benefit from touch and attention from others. Have you heard about the "wire monkey" experiments? They are slightly cruel, and I don't know if they would be approved if they were done now, but some fascinating experiments were done in the 1950s through the 1970s, particularly by Harry Harlow and his colleagues.

They took infant rhesus macaque monkeys, separated them from their mothers at birth, and did a number of experiments. The first finding was that primates raised in isolation, with no companions, did very poorly. They acted oddly, had more health problems, and did worse on almost every measure compared to monkeys with more social contact.

This finding makes some intuitive sense. If you look at how many governments and militaries torture people to gain information, they almost always put them in complete isolation. This in itself can be a form of torture and can break people down. In American prisons, the ultimate punishment is to put people into solitary confinement. When I was in training, I did some work in jails and prisons. My heart hurts when I remember some of the prisoners who spent long periods of time completely isolated. It was terrible, and I ultimately stopped doing this work because it was too painful to be a part of.

In contrast, having lots of social connections and spending time with loved ones can be nourishing and protective. A large U.S. survey study found that being well-integrated in a social community significantly predicts lower mortality rates, regardless of individuals' baseline physical health (Barger, 2013). More specifically, a compilation of nearly 150 studies revealed that individuals with social support live an average of 3.7 years longer than those who are less socially connected, irrespective of gender, baseline health quality, or ultimate cause of death (Holt-Lunstad et al., 2010). While it may be common knowledge that social support can help to reduce stress, one particularly clever study subjected men to a stress test after being offered no support, the support of their best friend, a nasal spray of the hormone oxytocin (which is typically released in connection with pair-bonding and physical affection), or a combination of social support and oxytocin. Levels of the stress hormone cortisol were lowest among those who were accompanied by a friend and received the oxytocin, which further supports the idea that positive close social ties can help buffer us from the negative effects of stress (Heinrichs et al., 2003). While *receiving* support is intuitively beneficial, being a good friend or partner to others may be even more protective. A study among older couples found that providing social support to friends, neighbors, relatives, and romantic partners significantly reduced risk of death (Brown et al., 2003).

The oxytocin and stress study alludes to another aspect of social connection that gets almost no publicity in classic therapy—the value of touch. In traditional talk therapy, we don't touch our patients. Sure, there might be a handshake (although some of my more psychodynamically inclined colleagues were shocked and appalled that I routinely shake my patients' hands!). In some cases, maybe a hug when treatment ends. But otherwise, there is essentially no touch in the therapeutic relationship. I suspect this is largely due to fears of lawsuits and not wanting to confuse the therapy relationship with a sexual relationship. I see merit in this idea. At the same time, it does lead to an emphasis on the value of words and talking that might de-emphasize how important touch can be for human beings.

If you go to the zoo and watch any chimpanzees or bonobos, you will see a lot of touching, or "grooming." We primates are wired to like touch. Some humans get enough touch and affection in their relationships with friends and lovers, but most don't. It's no surprise that we pay people to give us massages and to touch and cut our hair. Many people routinely get manicures and pedicures, in part because it feels nice to be touched and attended to. When we are not homophobically avoiding contact, we hug the people we care about regardless of gender, because touch feels good. When we touch another person (or gaze into their eyes), oxytocin is released in our brains. This helps us feel more connected to the other person and also feels pleasurable.

The most fascinating study involving wire monkeys was related to touch and contact. The dominant theory in the 1940s and 50s was that human mothers only mattered for the food they provided and that touch was not only unimportant for infant development, but even harmful. Orphanages studiously avoided touching the infants for fear of harming their development. Harlow and his scientists again separated infant rhesus monkeys from their mothers and made them choose between two monkey-shaped, man-made creations. One creation was a "wire monkey" made of wire and wood that had a bottle full of milk behind a nipple. It provided nutrition only, which was thought to be the only thing that mattered.

The other human-made creation was also made of wire and wood, but it was covered in terry cloth that was soft and could be hugged. This one had no source of milk. It only offered the opportunity for touch. In a startling discovery for that time, the infant monkeys almost exclusively favored the terry cloth "mothers." It turns out that touch does matter.

There are a few "ingredients" you need if you want to achieve optimal levels of connection with others. For one, you have to learn how to be vulnerable, which doesn't come naturally to most of us but is essential to all authentic human relationships. I could write about 20 pages on the awesomeness of vulnerability, but I think Brené Brown is more eloquent and knowledgeable than me, and I find her book *Daring Greatly* to be inspiring in this area. You also need to know how to talk to people and keep conversations going. There are a number of good resources in this department. The first that comes to mind is David Burns' book *Intimate Connections*. Any TEAM therapist can also help with this with a few hours of training. You also need a certain amount of "other-centeredness," which gets easier with practice by trying to make friends and can be strengthened through service.

The exciting news is that if you go out and form deep connections with other people, you get to reap numerous benefits. If you have affectionate friends and/or lovers, you can get an ample supply of touch and oxytocin. If you build up the courage to be vulnerable, you can feel close to people and have others feel close to you. When you are down, it feels wonderful to have people to turn to that you trust and respect. And although I believe we can be incredibly happy doing things by ourselves, sometimes it is wonderful to share experiences with others who we care about.

The point of this chapter is that if you were depressed, and primarily through reading this book and doing what it says you got to a place of experiencing the normal ups and downs of ordinary life—that is fantastic. This is a remarkable achievement.

You can also rise to the possibilities of an extraordinary life. You have read my writings about how life is short, it can have lots of suffering, we can expect to be disappointed frequently, and it's preferable to expect absolutely nothing. You might think I'm a pessimistic downer with low opinions of this earthly domain.

Nothing could be further from the truth! I am frequently amazed by how beautiful and rich life can be and the experiences that are possible for us. If we expect little and keep a curious and playful attitude, the world can be a glorious playground for us to explore. My wish for you is that you experience some combination of contentment, meaning, excitement, and connection. I wrote this for you because you are young, and there is still ample time for you to experience an amazing and beautiful life.

If this book makes even a small difference in your life and you recover from your depression, I would love to hear about it! Feel free to contact me. I get a high from feeling that I've helped someone, so I would love to know if your life was changed, or if you have any suggestions on how this could be better for future editions and future readers. I appreciate that you took the time to read this, and I wish you the best that life has to offer!

PATIENT HEALTH QUESTIONNAIRE-9 (PHQ-9)

Over the last 2 weeks, how often have you been bothered by any of the following problems? (Use "✔" to indicate your answer)	Not at all	Several days	More than half the days	Nearly every day
1. Little interest or pleasure in doing things	0	1	2	3
2. Feeling down, depressed, or hopeless	0	1	2	3
3. Trouble falling or staying asleep, or sleeping too much	0	1	2	3
4. Feeling tired or having little energy	0	1	2	3
5. Poor appetite or overeating	0	1	2	3
6. Feeling bad about yourself — or that you are a failure or have let yourself or your family down	0	1	2	3
7. Trouble concentrating on things, such as reading the newspaper or watching television	0	1	2	3
8. Moving or speaking so slowly that other people could have noticed? Or the opposite — being so fidgety or restless that you have been moving around a lot more than usual	0	1	2	3
9. Thoughts that you would be better off dead or of hurting yourself in some way	0	1	2	3

FOR OFFICE CODING ___0___ + _____ + _____ + _____

=Total Score: _____

If you checked off any problems, how difficult have these problems made it for you to do your work, take care of things at home, or get along with other people?

Not difficult at all	Somewhat difficult	Very difficult	Extremely difficult
☐	☐	☐	☐

Developed by Drs. Robert L. Spitzer, Janet B.W. Williams, Kurt Kroenke and colleagues, with an educational grant from Pfizer Inc. No permission required to reproduce, translate, display or distribute.

Cost-Benefit Analysis (CBA)

Thought to hold on to or Behavior to do:

_____

| Pros | Cons |

Last Resort Sleep Advice

Hello. If you are here and you have not done ALL of the guidelines in the previous chapters on sleep for at least two weeks, please go back to those other chapters and come back after you have done that.

The reason I am including this short section is that for a small number of you, even if you do perfect sleep hygiene, you will still struggle with insomnia and feeling tired.

Some of you have anxiety when you try to go to sleep, which keeps you up for a long time and causes low energy the next day. If this is you, you might benefit from a short course of Cognitive Behavioral Therapy for Insomnia (CBT-I). There are some excellent modules online, or you could go to a practitioner with expertise in this method. The general idea is that you might have worries about what will happen if you don't get enough sleep, and then, because you are so worried about that happening, you have trouble falling asleep and it becomes a self-fulfilling prophecy. Thankfully, this is changeable if you learn how to change your thoughts about sleeping.

Others might have a medical condition that causes you to be

sleepy during the day, even with impeccable sleep hygiene. The most common one is obstructive sleep apnea. I know more about this than I would prefer to know since I was recently diagnosed with it myself after being totally exhausted for six months.

If you have been following all of my previous suggestions completely and consistently for several weeks (including cutting out caffeine and naps completely and trying to get at least nine hours of sleep consistently) and you are still really tired, I would recommend that you get a sleep study. If you get one in a "sleep lab," they can diagnose many possible sleep conditions and can also recommend some treatment options. These overnight studies are not inexpensive (nor tremendously comfortable), but they can be excellent at diagnosing you and might be worth a shot if you are having consistent fatigue despite excellent sleep habits.

EXAMINE THE EVIDENCE

Thought: _____

Evidence For	Evidence Against
1.	1.
2.	2.
3.	3.
4.	4.

References

Ackard, D. M., Neumark-Sztainer, D., Story, M., & Perry, C. (2006). Parent-child connectedness and behavioral and emotional health among adolescents. *American Journal of Preventive Medicine, 30*(1), 59-66. doi: 10.1016/j.amepre.2005.09.013

American Academy of Pediatrics. (2014, August 25). Let Them Sleep: AAP Recommends Delaying Start Times of Middle and High Schools to Combat Teen Sleep Deprivation. *American Academy of Pediatrics.* Retrieved from https://www.aap.org/en-us/about-the-aap/aap-press-room/pages/let-them-sleep-aap-recommends-delaying-start-times-of-middle-and-high-schools-to-combat-teen-sleep-deprivation.aspx

Babyak, M., Blumenthal, J. A., Herman, S., Khatri, P., Doraiswamy, M., Moore, K., . . . Krishnan, K. R. (2000). Exercise treatment for major depression: maintenance of therapeutic benefit at 10 months. *Psychosomatic Medicine, 62*(5), 633-638.

Barger, S. D. (2013). Social integration, social support and mortality in the US National Health Interview Survey. *Psychosomatic Medicine, 75*(5), 510-517. doi: 10.1097/PSY.0b013e318292ad99

Barnes, A. (2007, January 20). The Happiest Man in the

World? *The Independent*. Retrieved from

http://www.independent.co.uk/news/uk/this-britain/the-happiest-

man-in-the-world-433063.html

Blumenthal, J. A., Babyak, M. A., Moore, K. A., Craighead, W. E.,

Herman, S., Khatri, P., . . . Krishnan, K. R. (1999). Effects of exercise

training on older patients with major depression. *Archives of Internal

Medicine, 159*(19), 2349-2356.

Borowsky, I. W., Ireland, M., & Resnick, M. D. (2001).

Adolescent suicide attempts: risks and protectors. *Pediatrics, 107*(3),

485-493.

Brown, S. L., Nesse, R. M., Vinokur, A. D., & Smith, D. M. (2003).

Providing social support may be more beneficial than receiving it:

results from a prospective study of mortality. *Psychological Science,

14*(4), 320-327.

Carter, O. L., Presti, D. E., Callistemon, C., Ungerer, Y., Liu, G. B.,

& Pettigrew, J. D. (2005). Meditation alters perceptual rivalry in Tibetan

Buddhist monks. *Current Biology, 15*(11), R412-413. doi:

10.1016/j.cub.2005.05.043

Condon, P., Desbordes, G., Miller, W. B., & DeSteno, D. (2013).

Meditation increases compassionate responses to suffering.

Psychological Science, 24(10), 2125-2127. doi:

10.1177/0956797613485603

Cooper, J., Kapur, N., Webb, R., Lawlor, M., Guthrie, E.,

Mackway-Jones, K., & Appleby, L. (2005). Suicide after deliberate self-

harm: a 4-year cohort study. *American Journal of Psychiatry, 162*(2),

297-303. doi: 10.1176/appi.ajp.162.2.297

Doyne, E. J., Ossip-Klein, D. J., Bowman, E. D., Osborn, K. M.,

McDougall-Wilson, I. B., & Neimeyer, R. A. (1987). Running versus

weight lifting in the treatment of depression. *Journal of Consulting and

Clinical Psychology, 55*(5), 748-754.

Flouri, E., & Buchanan, A. (2002). The protective role of parental

involvement in adolescent suicide. *Crisis, 23*(1), 17-22. doi:

10.1027//0227-5910.23.1.17

Fredrickson, B. L., Cohn, M. A., Coffey, K. A., Pek, J., & Finkel, S.

M. (2008). Open hearts build lives: positive emotions, induced through

loving-kindness meditation, build consequential personal resources.

Journal of Personality and Social Psychology, 95(5), 1045-1062. doi:

10.1037/a0013262

Goyal, M., Singh, S., Sibinga, E. M., Gould, N. F., Rowland-

Seymour, A., Sharma, R., . . . Haythornthwaite, J. A. (2014). Meditation programs for psychological stress and well-being: a systematic review and meta-analysis. *JAMA Internal Medicine, 174*(3), 357-368. doi: 10.1001/jamainternmed.2013.13018

Green, J. (2015, January 28). Palo Alto: Community searches for answers in wake of student suicides. *San Jose Mercury News*. Retrieved from http://www.mercurynews.com/my-town/ci_27409132/palo-alto-community-searches-answers-wake-student-suicides

Greenberg, P. E., Fournier, A. A., Sisitsky, T., Pike, C. T., & Kessler, R. C. (2015). The economic burden of adults with major depressive disorder in the United States (2005 and 2010). *The Journal of Clinical Psychiatry, 76*(2), 155-162. doi: 10.4088/JCP.14m09298

Harris, D., & Brady, E. (2011, July 28). Re-Wiring Your Brain for Happiness: Research Shows How Meditation Can Physically Change the Brain. *ABC News*. Retrieved from http://abcnews.go.com/US/meditation-wiring-brain-happiness/story?id=14180253

Harwood, D., Hawton, K., Hope, T., & Jacoby, R. (2001). Psychiatric disorder and personality factors associated with suicide in older people: a descriptive and case-control study. *International Journal of Geriatric Psychiatry, 16*(2), 155-165.

Heinrichs, M., Baumgartner, T., Kirschbaum, C., & Ehlert, U. (2003). Social support and oxytocin interact to suppress cortisol and subjective responses to psychosocial stress. *Biological Psychiatry, 54*(12), 1389-1398.

Henriksson, M. M., Aro, H. M., Marttunen, M. J., Heikkinen, M. E., Isometsa, E. T., Kuoppasalmi, K. I., & Lonnqvist, J. K. (1993). Mental disorders and comorbidity in suicide. *The American Journal of Psychiatry, 150*(6), 935-940. doi: 10.1176/ajp.150.6.935

Holt-Lunstad, J., Smith, T. B., & Layton, J. B. (2010). Social relationships and mortality risk: a meta-analytic review. *PLOS Medicine, 7*(7), e1000316. doi: 10.1371/journal.pmed.1000316

Kelly, W. E., Kelly, K. E., & Clanton, R. C. (2001). The relationship between sleep length and grade-point average among college students. *College Student Journal, 35*(1), 84–86.

Kessler, R. C., Barber, C., Birnbaum, H. G., Frank, R. G., Greenberg, P. E., Rose, R. M., . . . Wang, P. (1999). Depression in the workplace: effects on short-term disability. *Health Affairs, 18*(5), 163-171.

Kessler, R. C., Petukhova, M., Sampson, N. A., Zaslavsky, A. M., & Wittchen, H. U. (2012). Twelve-month and lifetime prevalence and lifetime morbid risk of anxiety and mood disorders in the United States. *International Journal of Methods in Psychiatric Research, 21*(3), 169-184. doi: 10.1002/mpr.1359

Lane, R. D., Reiman, E. M., Ahern, G. L., Schwartz, G. E., & Davidson, R. J. (1997). Neuroanatomical correlates of happiness, sadness, and disgust. *American Journal of Psychiatry, 154*(7), 926-933. doi: 10.1176/ajp.154.7.926

Lewinsohn, P. M., Hops, H., Roberts, R. E., Seeley, J. R., & Andrews, J. A. (1993). Adolescent psychopathology: I. Prevalence and incidence of depression and other DSM-III-R disorders in high school students. *Journal of Abnormal Psychology, 102*(1), 133-144.

Lim, D., Condon, P., & DeSteno, D. (2015). Mindfulness and compassion: an examination of mechanism and scalability. *PLOS One, 10*(2), e0118221. doi: 10.1371/journal.pone.0118221

Liou, S. (2010, June 26). Meditation and HD. *Huntington's Outreach Project for Education, At Stanford*. Retrieved from http://web.stanford.edu/group/hopes/cgi-bin/hopes_test/meditation-and-hd/#neuroscientists-and-buddhist-monks-results-of-an-unusual-collaboration

Lovato, N., & Gradisar, M. (2014). A meta-analysis and model of the relationship between sleep and depression in adolescents: recommendations for future research and clinical practice. *Sleep Medicine Reviews, 18*(6), 521-529. doi: 10.1016/j.smrv.2014.03.006

Lowe, B., Kroenke, K., Herzog, W., & Grafe, K. (2004). Measuring depression outcome with a brief self-report instrument: sensitivity to change of the Patient Health Questionnaire (PHQ-9). *Journal of Affective Disorders, 81*(1), 61-66. doi: 10.1016/S0165-0327(03)00198-8

Lutz, A., Greischar, L. L., Rawlings, N. B., Ricard, M., & Davidson, R. J. (2004). Long-term meditators self-induce high-amplitude gamma synchrony during mental practice. *Proceedings of the National Academy of Sciences of the United States of America, 101*(46), 16369-16373. doi: 10.1073/pnas.0407401101

Ma, S. H., & Teasdale, J. D. (2004). Mindfulness-based cognitive therapy for depression: replication and exploration of differential relapse prevention effects. *Journal of Consulting and Clinical Psychology, 72*(1), 31-40. doi: 10.1037/0022-006X.72.1.31

Mascaro, J. S., Rilling, J. K., Tenzin Negi, L., & Raison, C. L. (2013). Compassion meditation enhances empathic accuracy and related neural activity. *Social Cognitive and Affective Neuroscience, 8*(1), 48-55. doi: 10.1093/scan/nss095

Mathers, C., Fat, D. M., Boerma, J. T., & World Health

Organization. (2008). *The global burden of disease: 2004 update.*

Geneva, Switzerland: World Health Organization.

Mead, G. E., Morley, W., Campbell, P., Greig, C. A., McMurdo,

M., & Lawlor, D. A. (2009). Exercise for depression. *Cochrane Database*

Systematic Reviews (3), CD004366. doi:

10.1002/14651858.CD004366.pub4

Morgan, D. (2003). Mindfulness-based cognitive therapy for

depression: a new approach to preventing relapse. *Psychotherapy*

Research, 13(1), 123-125. doi: 10.1080/713869628

Ojakian, V., & Mukherjee, A. J. (2012, Oct 13). Analysis of 2009-

2011 Suicide Data of Santa Clara County: Suicide Prevention Initiative.

Santa Clara County Mental Health Department. Retrieved from

https://www.sccgov.org/sites/mhd/Providers/SuicidePrevention/Docu

ments/Analysis%20of%202009-

2011%20Suicide%20Data%20of%20SCC%2011-8.pdf

Short, M. A., Gradisar, M., Lack, L. C., & Wright, H. R. (2013). The

impact of sleep on adolescent depressed mood, alertness and academic

performance. *Journal of Adolescence, 36*(6), 1025-1033. doi:

10.1016/j.adolescence.2013.08.007

Sirois, F. M., & Tosti, N. (2012). Lost in the moment? An investigation of procrastination, mindfulness, and well-being. *Journal of Rational-Emotive and Cognitive-Behavior Therapy, 30*(4), 237-248.

Spitzer, R. L., Williams, J. B. W., & Kroenke, K. (n.d.). PATIENT HEALTH QUESTIONNAIRE-9 (PHQ-9). *Patient Health Questionnaire (PHQ) Screeners*. Retrieved from http://www.phqscreeners.com

Trivedi, M. H., Greer, T. L., Church, T. S., Carmody, T. J., Grannemann, B. D., Galper, D. I., . . . Blair, S. N. (2011). Exercise as an augmentation treatment for nonremitted major depressive disorder: a randomized, parallel dose comparison. *Journal of Clinical Psychiatry, 72*(5), 677-684. doi: 10.4088/JCP.10m06743

Wang, P. S., Beck, A. L., Berglund, P., McKenas, D. K., Pronk, N. P., Simon, G. E., & Kessler, R.C. (2004). Effects of major depression on moment-in-time work performance. *The American Journal of Psychiatry, 161*(10), 1885-1891.

Williamson, A. M., & Feyer, A. M. (2000). Moderate sleep deprivation produces impairments in cognitive and motor performance equivalent to legally prescribed levels of alcohol intoxication. *Occupational and Environmental Medicine, 57*(10), 649-655.

Made in the USA
San Bernardino, CA
08 June 2017